ISBN-13: 978-1514376980
ISBN-10: 1514376989

Set in PT Serif and Source Code Pro.

Cover design generated by:

https://github.com/qrohlf/trianglify-generator

"Python" and the Python logos are trademarks or registered trademarks of the Python Software Foundation, used by Dr. Jones with permission from the Foundation.

About the author

Martin trained as a biologist and started his programming career by learning Perl. He started teaching programming to other people shortly after that, and quickly branched out into other languages including Python. Since then he has taught programming to hundreds of beginners, specializing in courses for people without a traditional computer science background. His teaching philosophy is that programming courses must be friendly, approachable, and focussed on practical results.

Martin currently teaches programming in his position of Lecturer in Bioinformatics at Edinburgh University. He is the author of two previous programming books: *Python for Biologists* and *Advanced Python for Biologists*. This is his first programming book for a general audience.

You can get in touch with Martin at

martin@pythonforcompletebeginners.com

Table of Contents

5: Writing our own functions   115

6: Conditional tests   143

▌1: Introduction and environment

Welcome to Python

This book is an introduction to the Python programming language for complete beginners – those who have never written a program before, or who are just getting started with programming. Learning your first programming language is tricky, because you have to simultaneously learn about basic programming concepts and about the specifics of the language. Fortunately, Python is an excellent choice as a first language, for reasons we'll discuss below.

The goal of this book is to start with the absolute basics and get you to the point where you can confidently write your own programs from scratch. It will also give you the background to be able to seek out and understand more information on Python when you need it.

This introductory chapter contains important background information to help you get the most out of the book, so read it carefully. If you already have a system for writing and running Python programs, then feel free to skip the *Setting up your environment* section.

Why Python?

People who are new to programming tend to worry a lot about which language to learn. The choice of programming language does matter, of course, but it matters far less than people think it does. To put it another way, choosing the "wrong" programming language is very unlikely to mean the difference between failure and success when learning. Other factors (motivation, having time to devote to learning, helpful colleagues) are far more important, yet receive less attention.

The reason that people place so much weight on the *"what language should I learn?"* question is that it's a big, obvious question, and it's not difficult to find people who will give you strong opinions on the subject. It's also the first big question that beginners have to answer once they've decided to learn programming, so it assumes a great deal of importance in their minds.

There are a couple of reasons why choice of programming language is not as important as most people think it is. Firstly, nearly everybody who spends any significant amount of time programming will eventually end up using multiple languages. Partly this is just down to the simple constraints of various languages – if you want to write a web application you'll probably do it in Javascript, if you want to write a graphical user interface you'll probably use something like Java, and if you want to write low level algorithms you'll probably use C.

Secondly, learning a first programming language gets you 90% of the way towards learning a second, third, and fourth one. Learning to think like a programmer is largely a matter of learning to break down complex tasks into simple ones, and is a skill that cuts across all languages. So if you spend a few months learning Python and then discover that you really need to write in C, your time won't have been wasted as you'll be able to pick it up much quicker.

Having said all that, when learning to program we *do* need to pick a language to work in, so we should pick the one that will make the job of learning easiest. For most people, Python is that language. Here's why:

- It has a mostly consistent syntax, so you can generally learn one way of doing things and then apply it in multiple places

- It has a sensible set of built in libraries for doing lots of common tasks

- It is designed in such a way that there's an obvious way of doing most things

- It's one of the most widely used languages in the world, and there's a lot of advice, documentation and tutorials available on the web

- It's designed in a way that lets you start to write useful programs as soon as possible

- Its use of indentation, while annoying to people who aren't used to it, is great for beginners as it enforces a certain amount of readability

Another reason for choosing Python is that it's an extremely flexible language that's suitable for writing all sorts of programs. Python can be used for games, web applications, data analysis programs, graphical interfaces, home automation programs, and all sorts of other tasks. In other words, whatever type of program you're interested in writing, Python will probably be suitable.

How to use this book

Programming books generally fall into two categories; **reference** type books, which are designed for looking up specific bits of information, and **tutorial** type books, which are designed to be read cover to cover. This book is an example of the latter – code samples in later chapters often use material from previous ones, so you need to make sure you read the chapters in order. Exercises or examples from one chapter are sometimes used to illustrate the need for features that are introduced in the next.

There are a number of fundamental programming concepts that are relevant to material in multiple different chapters. In this book, rather than introduce these concepts all in one go, I've tried to explain them as they become necessary. This results in a tendency for earlier chapters to be longer than later ones, as they involve the introduction of more new concepts.

A certain amount of jargon is necessary if we want to talk about programs and programming concepts. I've tried to define each new technical term at the point where it's introduced, and then use it thereafter with occasional reminders of the meaning.

Chapters tend to follow a predictable structure. They generally start with a few paragraphs outlining the motivation behind the features that it will cover – why do they exist and what problems do they allow us to solve? These are followed by the main body of the chapter in which we discuss the relevant features and how to use them. The length of the chapters varies quite a lot – sometimes we want to cover a topic briefly, other times we need more depth. This section ends with a brief recap outlining what we have learned, followed by exercises and solutions (more on that topic below).

Formatting

A book like this has lots of special types of text – we'll need to look at examples of Python code and output, the contents of files, and technical terms. Take a minute to note the typographic conventions we'll be using:

In the main text of this book, **bold type** is used to emphasize important points and *italics* for technical terms and file names. Where code is mixed in with normal text it's written in a `monospaced font like this`. Occasionally there are footnotes[1] to provide additional information that is interesting to know but not crucial to understanding, or to give links to web pages.

---

1   Like this.

Example Python code is highlighted with a solid border and the name of the matching example file is written just underneath the example to the right:

```
Some example code goes here
```

example.py

Not every bit of code has a matching example file – much of the time we'll be building up a Python program bit by bit, in which case there will be a single example file containing the finished version of the program. The example files are in separate folders, one for each chapter, to make them easy to find.

Sometimes it's useful to refer to a specific line of code inside an example. For this, we'll use numbered circles like this❶:

```
a line of example code
another line of example code
this is the important line❶
here is another line
```

Example output (i.e. what we see on the screen when we run the code) is highlighted with a dotted border:

```
Some output goes here
```

Often we want to look at the code and the output it produces together. In these situations, you'll see a solid bordered code block followed immediately by a dotted bordered output block.

Other blocks of text (usually file contents) don't have any kind of border and look like this:

```
contents of a file
```

Often when looking at larger examples, or when looking at large amounts of output, we don't need to see the whole thing. In these cases, I'll use ellipses (...) to indicate that some text has been missed out.

I have used UK English spelling throughout, which I hope will not prove distracting to US readers.

In programming, we use different types of brackets for different purposes, so it's important to have different names for them. Throughout this book, I will use the word *parentheses* to refer to (), *square brackets* to refer to [], and *curly brackets* to refer to {}.

Exercises and solutions

The final part of each chapter is a set of exercises and solutions. The number and complexity of exercises differ greatly between chapters depending on the nature of the material. As a rule, early chapters have a large number of simple exercises, while later chapters have a small number of more complex ones. Many of the exercise problems are written in a deliberately vague manner and the exact details of how the solutions work is up to you (very much like real life programming!) You can always look at the solutions to see one possible way of tackling the problem, but there are often multiple valid approaches.

The exercises are probably the most important part of the book – when learning programming, it's vital that you practice writing programs from scratch rather than simply reading examples. I strongly recommend that you try tackling the exercises yourself before reading the solutions. I also encourage you to adopt an attitude of curious experimentation when working on the exercises – if you find yourself wondering if a particular variation on a problem is solvable, or if you recognize a closely related problem from your own work, try solving it! Continuous experimentation is a key part of developing as a programmer, and the quickest way to find out what a particular function or feature will do is to try it.

The example solutions to exercises are written in a different way to most programming textbooks: rather than simply present the finished solution, I have outlined the thought processes involved in solving the exercises and shown how the solution is built up step by step. Hopefully this approach will give you an insight into the problem solving mindset that programming requires. It's probably a good idea to read through the solutions even if you successfully solve the exercise problems yourself, as they sometimes suggest an approach that is not immediately obvious.

As with the code example files, the input files (for those exercises that use them) and the solutions are separated into different folders, one per chapter.

When learning to code, dealing with textbook exercises can be frustrating because it's often difficult to see the connection between the exercise problems and the type of programming you want to do. This is unfortunately unavoidable in a general programming book: different readers will have different programming goals so it's impossible to pick a set of exercises that will be relevant to everybody!

To help with this feeling, I've included a section at the end of each set of solutions entitled *What have we learned?* where I attempt to explain the relevance of the exercises to the wider world of programming. While you're working on the exercises, don't worry if they seem irrelevant – they have been designed to help you practice the skills you will need regardless of the types of programs you want to write.

Many of the exercises and examples are based around books by Charles Dickens, for no other reason than that book texts provide interesting data to work on, and are easily availably. You don't need to know anything about Charles Dickens or his books to understand the examples. However, if you're curious, it might be interesting to know that Charles Dickens was an English novelist working around 1850 and that his most popular books include *A Tale of Two Cities*, *Great Expectations* and *David Copperfield*.

Getting in touch

Learning to program is a difficult task, and my one goal in writing this book is to make it as easy and accessible as possible to get started. So, if you find anything that is hard to understand, or you think may contain an error, please get in touch – just drop me an email at

```
martin@pythonforcompletebeginners.com
```

and I promise to get back to you. If you find the book useful, then please also consider leaving an Amazon review to help other people find it.

Setting up your environment

All that you need in order to follow the examples and exercises in this book is a standard Python installation and a text editor. All the code in this book will run on either Linux, Mac or Windows machines. The slight differences between operating systems are explained in the text.

Python 2 vs. Python 3

As will quickly become clear if you spend any amount of time on the official Python website, there are two versions of Python currently available. The Python world is, at the time of writing, in the middle of a transition from version 2 to version 3. A discussion of the pros and cons of each version is well beyond the scope of this book[1], but here's what you need to know: install Python 3 if possible, but if you end up with Python 2, don't worry – all the code examples in the book will work with both versions.

If you're going to use Python 2, there is just one thing that you have to do in order to make some of the code examples work: include this line at the start of all your programs:

```
from __future__ import division
```

We won't go into the explanation behind this line, except to say that it's necessary in order to correct a small quirk with the way that Python 2 handles division of numbers.

Depending on what version you use, you might see slight differences between the output in this book and the output you get when you run the code on your computer. I've tried to note these differences in the text where possible.

Installing Python

The process of installing Python depends on the type of computer you're running on.

---

[1] You might encounter writing online that makes the 2 to 3 changeover seem like a big deal, and it is – but only for existing, large projects. When writing code from scratch, as you'll be doing when learning, you're unlikely to run into any problems.

If you're using **Windows**, start by going to this page:

```
https://www.python.org/downloads/windows/
```

then follow the link at the top of the page to the latest release. From here you can download and run the Windows installer.

If you're using **Mac OS X**, head to this page:

```
https://www.python.org/downloads/mac-osx/
```

then follow the link at the top of the page to the latest release. From here you can download and run the OS X installer.

If you're running a mainstream **Linux** distribution like Ubuntu, Python is probably already installed. If your Linux installation doesn't already have Python installed, try installing it with your package manager – the command will probably be either

```
sudo apt-get install python idle
```

or

```
sudo yum install python idle
```

Editing and running Python programs

In order to learn Python, we need two things: the ability to **edit** Python programs, and the ability to **run** them and view the output. There are two different ways to do this – using a text editor from the command line, or using Python's graphical editor program.

Using the command line

If you're already comfortable using the command line, then this will probably be the easiest way to get started. Firstly, you'll need to be able to open a new terminal. If you're using Windows, you can do this by running the *command prompt* program. If you're using OS X, run the *terminal* program from inside the *Utilities* folder. If you're using Linux, you probably already know how to open a new terminal – the program is probably called something like *Terminal Emulator*.

Since a Python program is just a text file, you can create and edit it with any text editor of your choice. Note that by a text editor I **don't** mean a word processor – do **not** try to edit Python programs with Microsoft Word, LibreOffice Writer, or similar tools, as they tend to insert special formatting marks that Python cannot read.

When choosing a text editor, there is one feature that is essential[1] to have, and one which is nice to have. The essential feature is something that's usually called *tab emulation*. The effect of this feature at first seems quite odd; when enabled, it replaces any tab characters that you type with an equivalent number of space characters (usually set to four). The reason why this is useful is discussed at length in chapter 4, but here's a brief explanation: Python is very fussy about your use of tabs and spaces, and unless you are very disciplined when typing, it's easy to end up with a mixture of tabs and spaces in your programs. This causes very infuriating problems, because they look the same to you, but not to Python! Tab emulation fixes the problem by making it effectively impossible for you to type a tab character.

---

1   OK, so it's not strictly essential, but you will find life much easer if you have it.

The feature that is nice to have is *syntax highlighting*. This will apply different colours to different parts of your Python code, and can help you spot errors more easily.

Recommended text editors are **Notepad++** for Windows[1], **TextWrangler** for Mac OSX[2], and **gedit** for Linux[3], all of which are freely available.

To run a Python program from the command line, just type the name of the Python executable (*python.exe* on Windows, *python* on OS X and Linux) followed by the name of the Python file you've created.

If any of the above doesn't work or seems complicated, just use the graphical editor as described in the next section.

Using a graphical editor

Python comes with a program called IDLE which provides a friendly graphical interface for writing and running Python code. IDLE is an example of an **Integrated Development Environment** (sometimes shortened to IDE).

IDLE works identically on Windows, OS X and Linux. To create a new Python file, just start the IDLE program and select *New File* from the *File* menu. This will open a new window in which you can type and edit Python code. When you want to run your Python program, use the *File* menu to save it (remember that the file name should end with .py) then select *Run Module* from the *Run* menu. The output will appear in the *Python Shell* window.

You can also use IDLE as a text editor – for example, to view input and output files. Just select *Open* from the *File* menu and pick the file that you

---

1   http://notepad-plus-plus.org/
2   http://www.barebones.com/products/TextWrangler/
3   https://projects.gnome.org/gedit/

want to view. To open a non-Python file, you'll have to select *All files* from the *Files of type* drop-down menu.

Downloading the files

You can download a zip file containing all the examples, exercise solutions and data files from this address:

```
http://pythonforcompletebeginners.com/exercises.zip
```

Before you go any further, download and extract the files so that you'll be able to follow along with the examples. There's a separate folder in the download for each chapter.

Reading the documentation

Part of the teaching philosophy that I've used in writing this book is that it's better to introduce a few useful features and functions rather than overwhelm you with a comprehensive list. The best place to go when you do want a complete list of the options available in Python is the official documentation

http://www.python.org/doc/

which, compared to many languages, is very readable. Chapter 8 contains a detailed overview of the documentation and how to use it.

2: Working with strings and numbers

Why are we so interested in working with text?

Open the first page of a book about learning Python[1], and the chances are that the first examples of code you'll see involve **numbers**. There's a good reason for that: numbers are generally simpler to work with than text – there are not too many things you can do with them (once you've got basic arithmetic out of the way) and so they lend themselves well to examples that are easy to understand. It's also a pretty safe bet that the average person reading a programming book is doing so because they need to do some number crunching.

The numbers-first approach makes a lot of sense for readers coming from a computer science or maths background, but it's not so good for the rest of us. Concentrating just on manipulating numbers leads to a lot of fairly boring examples and exercises that feel like we're just using Python as a calculator. So for this book, we're going to do things a bit differently: we'll start by playing around with a mixture of both text and numbers. This will allow us to look at more interesting examples and exercises, and to get more of a feel for how the language works.

I've hinted above that Python treats numbers and text differently. That's an important idea, and one that we'll return to in more detail later. For now, I want to introduce an important piece of jargon – the word *string*. String is the word we use to refer to a bit of text in a computer program (it just means a string of characters). From this point on we'll use the word *string* when we're talking about computer code.

---

1   Or indeed, any other programming language

Printing a message to the screen

The first thing we're going to learn is how to print a message to the screen. When we talk about *printing* text inside a computer program, we are not talking about producing a document on a printer. The word "print" is used for any occasion when our program outputs some text – in this case, the output is displayed in your terminal window or the output window of your IDE. Here's a line of Python code that will cause a friendly message to be printed. Quick reminder: solid lines indicate Python code, and dotted lines indicate the output.

```
print("Hello world")
```

hello_world.py

Let's take a look at the various bits of this line of code, and give some of them names:

The whole line is called a *statement*.

`print()` is the name of a *function*. The function tells Python, in vague terms, what we want to do – in this case, we want to print some text. The function name is always[1] followed by parentheses.

The bits of text inside the parentheses are called the *arguments* to the function. In this case, we just have one argument (later on we'll see examples of functions that take more than one argument, in which case the arguments are separated by commas).

The arguments tell Python what we want to do more specifically – in this case, the argument tells Python exactly what it is we want to print: a friendly greeting.

---

1   This is not strictly true, but it's easier to just follow this rule than worry about the exceptions.

Assuming you've followed the instructions in chapter 1 and set up your Python environment, type the line of code above into your favourite text editor or IDE, save it, and run it. You should see a single line of output like this:

```
Hello world
```

Quotes are important

In normal writing, we only surround a bit of text in quotes when we want to show that they are being spoken by somebody. In Python, however, strings are **always** surrounded by quotes. That is how Python is able to tell the difference between the instructions (like the function name) and the data (the thing we want to print). We can use either single or double quotes for strings – Python will happily accept either. The following two statements behave exactly the same:

```
print("Hello world")
print('Hello world')
```

different_quotes.py

Let's take a look at the output to prove it[1]:

```
Hello world
Hello world
```

You'll notice that the output above doesn't contain quotes – they are part of the code, not part of the string itself. If we **do** want to include quotes in

---

1   From this point on, I won't tell you to create a new file, enter the text, and run the program for each example – I will simply show you the output – but I encourage you to try the examples yourself.

the output, the easiest thing to do[1] is use the other type of quotes for surrounding the string:

```python
print("She said, 'Hello world'")
print('He said, "Hello world"')
```

printing_quotes.py

The above code will give the following output:

```
She said, 'Hello world'
He said, "Hello world"
```

Be careful when writing and reading code that involves quotes – you have to make sure that the quotes at the beginning and end of the string match up.

Use comments to annotate your code

Occasionally, we want to write some text in a program that is for humans to read, rather than for the computer to execute. We call this type of line a *comment*. To include a comment in your source code, start the line with a hash symbol[2]:

```python
# this is a comment, it will be ignored by the computer
print("Comments are very useful!")
```

comment.py

---

1   The alternative is to place a backslash character (\) before the quote – this is called *escaping* the quote and will prevent Python from trying to interpret it.

2   This symbol has many names – you might know it as number sign, pound sign, octothorpe, sharp (from musical notation), cross, or pig-pen.

You're going to see a lot of comments in the source code examples in this book, and also in the solutions to the exercises. Comments are a very useful way to document your code, for a number of reasons:

- You can put the explanation of what a particular bit of code does right next to the code itself. This makes it much easier to find the documentation for a line of code that is in the middle of a large program, without having to search through a separate document.

- Because the comments are part of the source code, they can never get mixed up or separated. In other words, if you are looking at the source code for a particular program, then you automatically have the documentation as well. In contrast, if you keep the documentation in a separate file, it can easily become separated from the code.

- Having the comments right next to the code acts as a reminder to update the documentation whenever you change the code. The only thing worse than undocumented code is code with old documentation that is no longer accurate!

Don't make the mistake, by the way, of thinking that comments are only useful if you are planning on showing your code to somebody else. When you start writing your own code, you will be amazed at how quickly you forget the purpose of a particular section or statement. If you are working on a solution to one of the exercises in this book on Friday afternoon, then come back to it on Monday morning, it will probably take you quite a while to pick up where you left off.

Comments can help with this problem by giving you hints about the purpose of code, meaning that you spend less time trying to understand your old code, thus speeding up your progress. A side benefit is that writing a comment for a bit of code reinforces your understanding at the time you are doing it. A good habit to get into is writing a quick one line comment above any line of code that does something interesting:

```
# print a friendly greeting
print("Hello world")
```

You'll see this technique used a lot in the code examples in this book, and I encourage you to use it for your own code as well.

Error messages and debugging

It may seem depressing early in the book to be talking about errors! However, it's worth pointing out at this early stage that **computer programs almost never work correctly the first time**. Programming languages are not like natural languages – they have a very strict set of rules, and if you break any of them, the computer will not attempt to guess what you intended, but instead will stop running and present you with an error message. You're going to be seeing a lot of these error messages in your programming career, so let's get used to them as soon as possible.

Forgetting quotes

Here's one possible error we can make when printing a line of output – we can forget to include the quotes:

```
print(Hello world)
```

missing_quotes.py

This is easily done, so let's take a look at the output we'll get if we try to run the above code[1]:

---

1   The output that you see might be very slightly different from this, depending on a bunch of

```
$ python error.py  File "error.py"❶, line 1❷
    print(Hello world)❸
                    ^
SyntaxError: invalid syntax
```

We can see that the name of the Python file is `error.py`❶ and that the error occurs on the first line of the file❷. Python's best guess at the location of the error is just before the close parentheses❸. Depending on the type of error, this can be wrong by quite a bit, so don't rely on it too much!

The type of error is a `SyntaxError`, which mean that Python can't understand the code – it breaks the rules in some way (in this case, the rule that strings must be surrounded by quotation marks). We'll see different types of errors later in this book.

Spelling mistakes

What happens if we misspell the name of the function?:

```
prin("Hello world")
```

spelling.py

We get a different type of error – a `NameError` – and the error message is a bit more helpful:

```
    prin("Hello world")❶
NameError: name 'prin' is not defined❷
```

---

factors like your operating system and the exact version of Python you are using.

This time, Python doesn't try to show us where on the line the error occurred, it just shows us the whole line❶. The error message tells us which word Python doesn't understand❷, so in this case, it's quite easy to fix.

Splitting a statement over two lines

What if we want to print some output that spans multiple lines? For example, we want to print the word "Hello" on one line and then the word "World" on the next line – like this:

```
Hello
World
```

We might try putting a new linc in the middle of our string like this:

```
print("Hello
World")
```

but that won't work and we'll get the following error message:

```
  File "error.py", line 1❶
    print("Hello
                 ^
SyntaxError: EOL while scanning string literal❷
```

Python finds the error when it gets to the end of the first line of code❶. The error message❷ is a bit more cryptic than the others. *EOL* stands for End Of Line, and *string literal* means a string in quotes. So to put this error message in plain English: *"I started reading a string in quotes, and I got to the end of the line before I came to the closing quotation mark"*

If splitting the line up doesn't work, then how do we get the output we want.....?

Printing special characters

The reason that the code above didn't work is that Python got confused about whether the new line was part of the *string* (which is what we wanted) or part of the *source code* (which is how it was actually interpreted). What we need is a way to include a new line as part of a string, and luckily for us, Python has just such a tool built in. To include a new line, we write a backslash followed by the letter n – Python knows that this is a special character and will interpret it accordingly. This special character is called a *newline*. Here's the code which prints "Hello world" across two lines:

```
# how to include a new line in the middle of a string
print("Hello\nworld")
```

print_newline.py

Notice that there's no need for a space before or after the newline. This newline character will become very important in the next chapter when we start reading data from files.

There are a few other useful special characters as well, all of which consist of a backslash followed by a letter. The only ones which you are likely to need for the exercises in this book are the *tab* character (\t) and the *carriage return* character (\r). The tab character can sometimes be useful when writing a program that will produce a lot of output. The carriage return character works a bit like a newline in that it puts the cursor back to the start of the line, but doesn't actually start a new line, so you can use it to overwrite output – this is sometimes useful for long running programs.

Storing strings in variables

OK, we've been playing around with the `print()` function for a while; let's introduce something new. We can take a string and assign a name to it using an equals sign – we call this a *variable*:

```
# store a greeting in the variable called my_greeting
my_greeting = "Hello!"
```

The variable `my_greeting` now points to the string `"Hello!"`. We call this *assigning* a variable, and once we've done it, we can use the variable name instead of the string itself – for example, we can use it in a `print()` statement[1]:

```
# store a greeting in the variable called my_greeting
my_greeting = "Hello!"

# now print the greeting
print(my_greeting)
```

print_variable.py

Notice that when we use the variable in a `print()` statement, we don't need any quotation marks – the quotes are part of the string, so they are already "built in" to the variable `my_greeting`. Also notice that this example includes a blank line to separate the different bits and make it easier to read. We are allowed to put as many blank lines as we like in our programs when writing Python – the computer will ignore them.

We can change the value of a variable as many times as we like once we've created it:

---

1   If it's not clear why this is useful, don't worry – it will become much more apparent when we look at some longer examples.

```
my_greeting = "Hello!"
print(my_greeting)

# change the value of my_greeting
my_greeting = "Hi, friend!"
```

Here's a very important point that trips many beginners up: variable names are **arbitrary** – that means that we can pick **whatever we like** to be the name of a variable. So our code above would work in exactly the same way if we picked a different variable name:

```
# store a greeting in the variable banana
banana = "Hello!"

# now print the greeting
print(banana)
```

What makes a good variable name? Generally, it's a good idea to use a variable name that gives us a clue as to what the variable refers to. In this example, my_greeting is a good variable name, because it tells us what kind of information is stored in the variable. Conversely, banana is a bad variable name, because it doesn't really tell us anything about the value that's stored. As you read through the code examples in this book, you'll get a better idea of what constitutes good and bad variable names.

This idea – that names for things are arbitrary, and can be anything we like – is a theme that will occur many times in this book, so it's important to keep it in mind. Occasionally you will see a variable name that **looks like** it has some sort of relationship with the value it points to:

```
my_file = "my_file.txt"
```

but don't be fooled! Variable names and strings are separate things.

I said above that variable names can be anything we want, but it's actually not quite that simple – there are some rules we have to follow. We are only allowed to use letters, numbers, and underscores, so we can't have variable names that contain odd characters like £, ^ or %. We are not allowed to start a name with a number (though we can use numbers in the middle or at the end of a name). Finally, we can't use a word that's already built in to the Python language like "print".

It's also important to remember that variable names are case sensitive, so `my_greeting`, `MY_GREETING` and `My_Greeting` are all separate variables. Technically this means that you could use all three names in a Python program to store different values, but please don't do this – it is very easy to become confused when you use very similar variable names.

Tools for manipulating strings

Now we know how to store and print strings, we can take a look at a few of the facilities that Python has for manipulating them. In the exercises at the end of this chapter, we'll look at how we can use multiple different tools together in order to carry out more complex operations.

Concatenation

We can concatenate (stick together) two strings using the + symbol[1]. This symbol will join together the string on the left with the string on the right:

```
my_greeting = "Hel" + "lo"
print(my_greeting)
```

`print_concatenated.py`

---

1   We call this the *concatenation operator*.

Let's take a look at the output:

```
Hello
```

In the above example, the things being concatenated were strings, but we can also use variables that point to strings:

```
first_part = "Hel"
my_greeting = first_part + "lo"
# my_greeting is now "Hello"
```

We can even join multiple strings together in one go:

```
first_word = "Hello"
second_word = "World"
my_greeting = first_word + " " + second_word
# my_greeting is now "Hello World"
```

Notice in this last example how the middle string is a single space character. Although in everyday writing we think of a space as just a gap between two words, in programming a space is a character just like any other.

It's important to realize that the result of concatenating two strings together is itself a string. So it's perfectly OK to use a concatenation inside a print() statement, for example:

```
print("Hello" + " " + "world")
```

As we'll see in the rest of the book, using one tool inside another is quite a common thing to do in Python.

Finding the length of a string

Another useful built in tool in Python is the `len()` function (`len` is short for length). Just like `print()`, `len()` takes a single argument (take a quick look back at when we were discussing the `print()` function for a reminder about what arguments are) which is a string. However, the behaviour of the `len()` function is quite different. Instead of outputting text to the screen, `len()` outputs a value that can be stored – we call this the *return value*. In other words, if we write a program that uses `len()` to calculate the length of a string, the program will run but we won't see any output:

```
# this line doesn't produce any output
len("Hello World")
```

If we want to actually use the return value, we need to store it in a variable, and then do something useful with it (like printing it):

```
greeting_length = len("Hello world!")
print(greeting_length)
```

print_length.py

There's another interesting thing about the `len()` function: the result (or *return value*) is not a string, it's a number. This is a very important idea so I'm going to write it out in bold: **Python treats strings and numbers differently.**

We can see that this is the case if we try to concatenate together a number and a string. Consider this short program which calculates the length of my name and then prints out a message telling us the length:

```
# store my name in a variable
my_name = "Martin"

# calculate the length of my name and store it in a variable
name_length = len(my_name)

# print a message telling us the length of the name
("The length of the name is " + name_length)
```

When we try to run this program, we get the following error:

```
    print("The length of the name is " + name_length)
TypeError: cannot concatenate 'str' and 'int' objects❶
```

The error message❶ is short but informative: "cannot concatenate 'str' and 'int' objects". Python is complaining that it doesn't know how to concatenate a **string** (which it calls str for short) and a **number** (which it calls int – short for integer). Strings and numbers are examples of *data types* – different kinds of information that can exist inside a program.

Happily, Python has a built in solution to this problem – a function called str() which turns a number[1] into a string so that we can print it. Here's how we can modify our program to use it – I've removed the comments from this version to make it a bit more compact:

```
my_name = "Martin"
name_length = len(my_name)
print("The length of the name is " + str(name_length))
```

print_name_length.py

---

1   Or a value of any non-string type, but we'll come to that later.

The only thing we have changed is that we've replaced `name_length` with `str(name_length)` inside the `print()` statement[2]. Notice that because we're using one function (`str()`) inside another function (`print()`), our statement now ends with two closing parentheses.

Let's take a moment to refresh our memory of all the new terms we've learned by writing out what we need to know about the `str()` function:

> `str()` is a *function* which takes one *argument* (whose type is *number*), and *returns* a value (whose type is *string*) representing that number.

If you're unsure about the meanings of any of the words in italics, skip back to the earlier parts of this chapter where we discussed them. Understanding how types work is key to avoiding many of the frustrations which new programmers typically encounter, so make sure the idea is clear in your mind before moving on with the rest of this book.

Sometimes we need to go the other way – we have a string that we need to turn into a number. The function for doing this is called `int()`, which is short for integer. It takes a string as its argument and returns a number:

```
number = 3 + int('4')
# number is now 7
```

We won't need to use `int()` for a while, but once we start reading information from files later on in the book it will become very useful.

Changing case

We can convert a string to lower case by using a new type of tool – a *method* that belongs to strings. A *method* is like a *function*, but instead of being built in to the Python language, it belongs to a particular *type*. The

---

2   If you experiment with some of the code here, you might discover that you can also print a number directly without using `str` – but only if you don't try to concatenate it.

method we are talking about here is called `lower()`, and we say that it belongs to the *string* type. Here's how we use it:

```
my_name = "MARTIN"
# print my_name in lower case
print(my_name.lower())
```

`print_lower.py`

Notice how using a method looks different to using a function. When we use a function like `print()` or `len()`, we write the function name first and the arguments go in parentheses:

```
print("Hello")
len(my_name)
```

When we use a method, we write the name of the variable first, followed by a period, then the name of the method, then the method arguments in parentheses. For the example we're looking at here, `lower()`, there is no argument, so the opening and closing parentheses are right next to each other.

It's important to notice that the `lower()` method does **not** actually change the variable; instead it returns a **copy** of the variable in lower case. We can prove that it works this way by printing the variable before and after running `lower()`. Here's the code to do so:

```
my_name = "MARTIN"
# print the variable
print("before: " + my_name)

# run the lower method and store the result
lowercase_name = my_name.lower()

# print the variable again
print("after: " + my_name)
```

print_before_and_after.py

and here's the output we get:

```
before: MARTIN
after: MARTIN
```

Just like the len() function, in order to actually do anything useful with the lower() method, we need to store the result (or print it right away).

Because the lower() method belongs to the string type, we can only use it on variables that are strings. If we try to use it on a number:

```
my_number = len("Martin")
# my_number is 6
print(my_number.lower())
```

we will get an error that looks like this:

```
AttributeError: 'int' object has no attribute 'lower'
```

The error message is a bit cryptic, but hopefully you can grasp the meaning: something that is a number (an int, or integer) does not have a lower() method. This is a good example of the importance of types in Python code: **we can only use methods on the type that they belong to**.

Before we move on, let's just mention that there is another method that belongs to the string type called upper() – you can probably guess what it does!

Replacement

Here's another example of a useful method that belongs to the string type: replace(). replace() is slightly different from anything we've seen before – it takes two arguments (both strings) and returns a copy of the variable where all occurrences of the first string are replaced by the second string. That's quite a long winded description, so here are a few examples to make things clearer:

```python
greeting = "Hi, friend!"

# replace i with o
print(greeting.replace("i", "o"))

# we can replace more than one character
print(greeting.replace("Hi", "Howdy"))

# the original variable is not affected
print(greeting)
```

replace.py

And this is the output we get:

```
Ho, froend!
Howdy, friend!
Hi, friend!
```

Notice how the first replacement has replaced both of the **i** characters – the one that's part of the word "Hi" and also the one that's part of the word "friend".

Extracting part of a string

What do we do if we have a long string, but we only want a short portion of it? This is known as taking a *substring*, and it has its own notation in Python. To get a substring, we follow the variable name with a pair of square brackets which enclose a start and stop position, separated by a colon. Again, this is probably easier to visualize with a couple of examples – let's start with a long word and extract some bits of it:

```python
word = "spontaneous"

# print letters three to five
print(word[3:5])

# positions start at zero, not one
print(word[0:4])

# if we leave out the stop position it goes to the end of the string
print(word[5:])
```

print_substrings.py

and here's the output:

```
nt
spon
aneous
```

There are two important things to notice here. Firstly, we actually start counting from position zero, rather than one – in other words, position 3 is actually the fourth character[1]. This explains why the first character of the first line of output is **n** and not **o** as you might think. Secondly, the positions are **inclusive** at the start, but **exclusive** at the stop. In other words, the expression word[3:5] gives us everything starting at the

---

1 This seems very annoying when you first encounter it, but we'll see later why it's necessary.

fourth character, and stopping just before the sixth character (i.e. characters four and five).

If we just give a single number in the square brackets, we'll just get a single character:

```
word = "spontaneous"
first_letter = word[0]
```

We'll learn a lot more about this type of notation, and what we can do with it, in chapter 4.

Counting and finding substrings

A common job in programming is to count the number of times some pattern occurs in a bit of text. In computer programming terms, what that translates to is counting the number of times a *substring* occurs in a *string*. The method that does the job is called count(). It takes a single argument whose type is string, and returns the number of times that the argument is found in the variable. The return type is a number, so we must be careful about how we use it!

Let's use our favourite word "spontaneous" again as an example. Remember that we have to use our old friend str() to turn the counts into strings so that we can print them.

```
word = "spontaneous"

# count some different letters
n_count = word.count('n')
ne_count = word.count('ne')
x_count = word.count('x')

# now print the counts
print("number of n's: " + str(n_count))
print("number of ne's: " + str(ne_count))
print("number of x's: " + str(x_count))
```

count_letters.py

The output shows how the count() method behaves:

```
number of n's: 2
number of ne's: 1
number of x's: 0
```

Counting the number of **n**'s gives us an answer of two. Counting the number of **ne**'s gives us one, because only one of the **n**'s is followed by a letter **e**. And counting the number of **x**'s gives us the answer zero, because there's no letter **x** in the word.

A closely related problem to counting substrings is finding their location. What if instead of counting the number of **n** letters in our word we want to know where they are? The find() method will give us the answer, at least for simple cases. find() takes a single string argument, just like count(), and returns a number which is the position at which that substring first appears in the string (in computing, we call that the *index* of the substring).

Remember that in Python we start counting from zero rather than one, so position 0 is the first character, position 4 is the fifth character, etc. A couple of examples:

```
word = "spontaneous"
print(str(word.find('n')))
print(str(word.find('ne')))
print(str(word.find('x')))
```

find_letters.py

And the output:

```
3
6
-1
```

A couple of interesting things to notice here: when we ask for the location of the letter **n**, we get back the first position where it occurs, and when we ask for the location of a substring that doesn't exist, we get back the answer -1.

Of the tools we've discussed in this section, three – `replace()`, `count()` and `find()` – require at least two strings to work, so be careful that you don't get confused about the order. Remember that:

```
word.count(letter)
```

is **not** the same as:

```
letter.count(word)
```

Recap

We started this chapter talking about strings and how to work with them, but along the way we had to take a lot of diversions, all of which were necessary to understand how the different string tools work. Thankfully, that means that we've covered most of the nuts and bolts of the Python language, which will make future chapters go much more smoothly.

We've learned about some general features of the Python programming language like

- the difference between *functions*, *statements* and *arguments*

- the importance of *comments* and how to use them

- how to use Python's error messages to fix bugs in our programs

- how to store *values* in *variables*

- the way that *types* work, and the importance of understanding them

- the difference between *functions* and *methods*, and how to use them both

And we've encountered some tools that are specifically for working with strings:

- concatenation

- different types of quotes

- special characters

- changing the case of a string

- finding and counting substrings

- replacing bits of a string with something new

- extracting bits of a string to make a new string

Many of the general features will crop up again in future chapters, and will be discussed in more detail, but you can always return to this chapter if you want to brush up on the basics. The exercises for this chapter will allow you to practice using the string manipulation tools and to become familiar with them. They'll also give you the chance to practice builder bigger programs by using the individual tools as building blocks.

Exercises

Reminder: the descriptions of the exercises are brief and may be kind of ambiguous – just like requirements for programs you will write in real life! Try the exercises yourself before you look at the solutions, but make sure to read the solutions even if you find the exercises easy, as they contain extra details that may be useful.

Counting vowels

Here's the first sentence of *A Tale of Two Cities*, by Charles Dickens (who was fond of long sentences!):

```
It was the best of times, it was the worst of times, it was the
age of wisdom, it was the age of foolishness, it was the epoch
of belief, it was the epoch of incredulity, it was the season of
Light, it was the season of Darkness, it was the spring of hope,
it was the winter of despair, we had everything before us, we
had nothing before us, we were all going direct to Heaven, we
were all going direct the other way - in short, the period was
so far like the present period, that some of its noisiest
authorities insisted on its being received, for good or for
evil, in the superlative degree of comparison only.
```

What proportion of this sentence is made up of the vowels (a,e,i,o and u)? Write a program that will calculate the answer and print it out.

Hint: you can use normal mathematical symbols like add (+), subtract (-), multiply (*), divide (/) and parentheses to carry out calculations on numbers in Python.

Reminder: if you're using Python 2 rather than Python 3, include this line at the top of your program:

```
from __future__ import division
```

to make sure that division will work correctly.

Swapping letters

Here's another first sentence, this time from *Oliver Twist*.

```
emong othar public buildings in e cartein town, which for meny
raesons it will ba prudent to rafrein from mantioning, end to
which i will essign no fictitious nema, thara is ona enciantly
common to most towns, graet or smell: to wit, e workhousa; end
in this workhousa wes born; on e dey end deta which i naad not
troubla mysalf to rapaet, inesmuch es it cen ba of no possibla
consaquanca to tha raedar, in this stega of tha businass et ell
avants; tha itam of mortelity whosa nema is prafixad to tha haed
of this cheptar.
```

Unfortunately, some of the letters have got mixed up; the **a**'s and the **e**'s have been swapped[1]. Write a program that will fix this and print out the correct text (it should start: "among other public buildings in a certain town...")

Sentence lengths

Here is the opening paragraph from *The Old Curiosity Shop*:

```
Night is generally my time for walking. In the summer I often
leave home early in the morning, and roam about fields and lanes
all day, or even escape for days or weeks together; but, saving
in the country, I seldom go out until after dark, though, Heaven
be thanked, I love its light and feel the cheerfulness it sheds
upon the earth, as much as any creature living.
```

---

1   For this exercise I've put the entire text in lower case, just to prevent things from becoming
     too complicated.

The paragraph is made up of two sentences. We can see that the first sentence is short and the second one is long, but what are their actual lengths? Write a program that will calculate the lengths and print them out.

Place name, part one

Here's the first line of *Little Dorrit*:

```
Thirty years ago, Marseilles lay burning in the sun, one day.
```

It mentions the name of a city. The name of the city starts at the 19th character of the sentence and ends at the 28th character. Write a program that uses these numbers to extract just the name of the city from the sentence and print it.

Place name, part two

Using the information from part one, write a program that will calculate what percentage of the sentence is made up of the name of the city.

Reminder: if you're using Python 2 rather than Python 3, include this line at the top of your program:

```
from __future__ import division
```

Place name, part three

Using the information from part one, write a program that will print out the original sentence but with the name of the city in upper case.

Solutions

Counting vowels

This exercise is going to involve a mixture of strings and numbers. The actual math here is straightforward; we just need to count the number of times each vowel occurs, add them all together, and divide by the total length of the string.

There are six numbers we need to figure out: the number of times each of the five vowels occurs and the length of the string. We know that we can get the length of the string using the len() function, and we can count the number of times a given letter occurs using the count() method. Rather than typing out the long sentence, we can just copy and paste it into our code. Here's a few lines of code to figure out the vowel counts and the length:

```
sentence = "It was the best of times, it was the worst of times, it was
the age of wisdom, it was the age of foolishness, it was the epoch of
belief, it was the epoch of incredulity, it was the season of Light, it
was the season of Darkness, it was the spring of hope, it was the winter
of despair, we had everything before us, we had nothing before us, we
were all going direct to Heaven, we were all going direct the other way
- in short, the period was so far like the present period, that some of
its noisiest authorities insisted on its being received, for good or for
evil, in the superlative degree of comparison only."

length = len(sentence)
a_count = sentence.count('a')
e_count = sentence.count('e')
i_count = sentence.count('i')
o_count = sentence.count('o')
u_count = sentence.count('u')
```

Notice that the bit of code where we store the sentence in a variable
wraps across multiple lines. This is just to make it fit on the page – in fact
it's a single statement.

At this point, it seems sensible to check these lines before we go any
further. So rather than diving straight in and doing some calculations,
let's print out these numbers so that we can see if they look
approximately right. We'll have to remember to turn the numbers into
strings using str() so that we can print them. To make it easier to read,
we'll use ... to represent the middle bit of the text:

```
sentence = "It was ... comparison only."

length = len(sentence)
a_count = sentence.count('a')
e_count = sentence.count('e')
i_count = sentence.count('i')
o_count = sentence.count('o')
u_count = sentence.count('u')

print("number of a's : " + str(a_count))
print("number of e's : " + str(e_count))
print("number of i's : " + str(i_count))
print("number of o's : " + str(o_count))
print("number of u's : " + str(u_count))
```

Let's take a look at the output from this program:

```
number of a's : 28
number of e's : 69
number of i's : 44
number of o's : 44
number of u's : 5
```

That looks about right, but how do we know if it's exactly right? We could
go through the sentence manually one letter at a time, and verify that
there are twenty-eight a's etc., but that doesn't seem like a great use of

our time. A better idea is to run the exact same code with a much shorter test string, to verify that it works before going ahead and running it on the longer string.

Here's a version that uses a very short test string with one of each of the five vowels, and five random consonants:

```
sentence = "aeiouftxdw"

length = len(sentence)
a_count = sentence.count('a')
e_count = sentence.count('e')
i_count = sentence.count('i')
o_count = sentence.count('o')
u_count = sentence.count('u')

print("number of a's : " + str(a_count))
print("number of e's : " + str(e_count))
print("number of i's : " + str(i_count))
print("number of o's : " + str(o_count))
print("number of u's : " + str(u_count))
```

and here's the output:

```
number of a's : 1
number of e's : 1
number of i's : 1
number of o's : 1
number of u's : 1
```

Everything looks OK – we can probably go ahead and run the code on the long sentence. But wait; we know that the next step is going to involve doing some calculations using the numbers. If we switch back to the long sentence now, then we'll be in the same position as we were before – we'll end up with an answer for the proportion of vowels, but we won't know if it's the right one.

A better plan is to stick with the short test sentence until we've written the whole program, and check that we get the right answer for the proportion of vowels (we can easily see by glancing at the test sentence that half of the characters are vowels, so our answer should be 0.5). Here goes – we'll use the add and divide symbols from the exercise hint:

```
from __future__ import division

sentence = "aeiouftxdw"

length = len(sentence)
a_count = sentence.count('a')
e_count = sentence.count('e')
i_count = sentence.count('i')
o_count = sentence.count('o')
u_count = sentence.count('u')
proportion = a_count + e_count + i_count + o_count + u_count / length
print("proportion of vowels is " + str(proportion))
```

The output from this program looks like this:

```
proportion of vowels is 4.1
```

That doesn't look right. Looking back at the code we can see what has gone wrong – in the calculation, the division has taken precedence over the addition, so only the u_count has been divided by the length. To fix it, we need to add some parentheses around the addition, so that the line becomes:

```
proportion = (a_count + e_count + i_count + o_count + u_count) / length
```

Now we get the correct output for the test sentence:

```
proportion of vowels is 0.5
```

and we can go ahead and run the program using the longer sentence, confident that the code is working and that the calculations are correct.

There's one final problem waiting to trip us up: did you notice that the long sentence starts with an upper case **I**? Because the argument to count is in lower case:

```
i_count = sentence.count('i')
```

the first **I** will not be included. We could do separate counts for upper and lower case versions of each letter, but an easier fix is to make a version of the sentence that's all in lower case, then do the counting on it. Here's the final solution:

```
from __future__ import division

sentence = "It was the ... comparison only."
low_sentence = sentence.lower()
length = len(sentence)

# make counts for all the vowels
a_count = low_sentence.count('a')
e_count = low_sentence.count('e')
i_count = low_sentence.count('i')
o_count = low_sentence.count('o')
u_count = low_sentence.count('u')

# use the counts to calculate the proportion
proportion = (a_count + e_count + i_count + o_count + u_count) / length
print("proportion of vowels is " + str(proportion))
```

count_vowels.py

and the final output:

```
proportion of vowels is 0.311582381729
```

Swapping letters

This one seems pretty straightforward – we need to take our sentence and replace **a** with **e** and **e** with **a**. We'll have to make two separate calls to `replace()`, and use the return value for each on as the input for the next one. Let's try it:

```
sentence = "emong othar public buildings in e cartein ... cheptar."

replace_one = sentence.replace('a', 'e')
replace_two = replace_one.replace('e', 'a')

print(replace_two)
```

When we take a look at the output, however, something seems wrong:

```
among othar public buildings in a cartain ... chaptar.
```

Just look at the last word. In the original text this was "cheptar", so in the final result the **e** and the **a** should have both been swapped to leave us with "chapter". However, what has actually happened is that both vowels have ended up as **a**. This is definitely not what we want!

Let's try and track the problem down by printing out the intermediate step as well:

```
sentence = "Among othar public buildings in e cartein ...  cheptar. "

print(sentence)
replace_one = sentence.replace('a', 'e')
print(replace_one)
replace_two = replace_one.replace('e', 'a')
print(replace_two)
```

The output from this program makes it clear what the problem is:

```
emong othar public buildings in e cartein ... cheptar.
emong other public buildings in e certein ... chepter.
emong othar public buildings in a cartain ... chaptar.
```

Again, look at the final word. The first replacement (the result of which is shown in the second line of the output) works fine – the **a** gets replaced with **e**. The second replacement is where it starts to go wrong: both of the **e**'s are replaced with **a**, including the one that is there as a result of the first replacement. So during the two replacements, the second to last character of "cheptar" is changed from **a** to **e** and then straight back to **a** again.

How are we going to get round this problem? One option is to pick a temporary intermediate character for characters that are originally **a** and which we want to be **e** in the final output. For example, we could first replace **a** with **z**, then later on replace **z** with **e**:

```
sentence = "emong othar public buildings ... cheptar."
replace_one = sentence.replace('a', 'z')
replace_two = replace_one.replace('e', 'a')
replace_three = replace_two.replace('z', 'e')
print(replace_three)
```

This gets us the result we are looking for:

```
among other public buildings in a certain ... chapter.
```

It avoids the problem with the previous program by using another letter to stand in for the letter **a** while the replacements are being done. Notice that this only works because the temporary letter we chose – **z** – doesn't appear anywhere in the sentence. If we tried the same approach with an intermediate letter that **does** appear in the sentence then we would end up changing that letter to **e** in the final output as well. If we had to solve the same problem for the whole book, then it would be difficult because we'd be unlikely to be able to find a letter that didn't occur anywhere in the whole book!

Here's a slightly more elegant way of doing it. We can take advantage of the fact that the `replace()` method is case sensitive and make the replacements in upper case. Then, once both the replacements have been carried out, we can simply call `lower()` and change the whole sentence back to lower case. Let's take a look at how this works:

```python
sentence = "emong othar public buildings in e cartein ... cheptar."
print(sentence)

# do the replacements in upper case
replace_one = sentence.replace('a', 'E')
print(replace_one)
replace_two = replace_one.replace('e', 'A')
print(replace_two)

# convert to lower case and print
print(replace_two.lower())
```

swap_vowels.py

The output lets us see exactly what's happening – notice that in this version of the program we print the final string twice, before and after being converted to lower case:

```
emong othar public buildings in e cartein ... cheptar.
emong othEr public buildings in e cErtein ... cheptEr.
Among othEr public buildings in A cErtAin ... chAptEr.
among other public buildings in a certain ... chapter.
```

We can see what happens as the program runs. First, all lower case **a**'s are replaced with upper case **E**'s. Then all lower case **e**'s are replaced with upper case **A**'s. Finally, the whole thing is converted to lower case.

Sentence lengths

Let's start this exercise by solving the problem manually. If we look at the first bit of the sentence:

```
Night is generally my time for walking. In the summer ...
```

We can spot the boundary between the two sentences quite easily – it's the period at the end of the word "walking". A quick count tells us that there are 32 letters in the first sentence, so we might be tempted to give that as the answer. However, remember that in programming, spaces are counted as part of the length of a string just like any other character, so we need to include the 6 spaces, giving a total of 38 characters.

Now we come to an interesting question: do we want to include the period as part of the sentence length? The exercise didn't say, so we have to make our own mind up! For the purposes of this solution, we'll say that we do, so the total length of the first sentence is 39 characters. We could now go on and calculate the length of the entire passage and subtract 39 from it to get the length of the second sentence.

Writing a program to figure out the lengths of the sentences is just a question of applying the same logic. We'll use the `find()` method to figure out the position of the period❶, then add one to account for the fact that the positions start counting from zero – this will give us the length of the first sentence. From there we can get the length of the second sentence by finding the length of the whole paragraph and subtracting the length of the first sentence❷:

```
text = "Night is generally ... any creature living."

period_position = text.find(".")❶
first_length = period_position + 1
second_length = len(text) - first_length❷

print("First sentence is " + str(first_length) + " characters long")
print("Second sentence is " + str(second_length) + " characters long")
```

sentence_lengths.py

The output from this program confirms that it agrees with the answer we got manually:

```
First sentence is 39 characters long
Second sentence is 328 characters long
```

It's worth pausing for a moment to consider how flexible this program is – would it work on any text, or just the one that we're using in this example? If we think about it, it becomes clear that the program will work for any piece of text that's made up of exactly two sentences – pick one and try it!

Place name, part one

In this exercise, we're being asked to produce a program that extracts a particular section of text based on the positions where it stops and starts. We can begin by storing the sentence in a variable:

```
sen = "Thirty years ago, Marseilles lay burning in the sun, one day."
```

Now we can use the substring notation from earlier in the chapter to get the bit of text we want. It says in the exercise description that the city name goes from the 19th to the 28th character, so we might be tempted to try this:

```
city_name = sen[19:28]
print(city_name)
```

However, remember that when we're counting positions in Python we start counting at zero rather than one, so this attempt misses out the first letter:

```
arseilles
```

We can try to fix this by subtracting one from the start and stop positions:

```
city_name = sen[18:27]
print(city_name)
```

But now we're missing the last letter:

```
Marseille
```

because positions include the start, but exclude the end. The correct set of numbers is this:

```
sen = "Thirty years ago, Marseilles lay burning in the sun, one day."
city_name = sen[18:28]
print(city_name)
```

place_name_1.py

Although the solution is very simple, this exercise emphasizes the point that we have to be very careful when translating human language instructions (which are often vague and open to interpretation) to programming language instructions (which are always completely unambiguous).

Place name, part two

To calculate the percentage of the sentence which is made up of the city name, we need to divide the length of the city name by the length of the entire sentence and multiply by 100. There are two different ways to get the length of the city name[1]. We could just use the positions of the start and the the end of the name to figure out the length. However, since we've already written the code to extract the city name, we can simply measure its length using the `len()` ❶ function:

```
from __future__ import division
sen = "Thirty years ago, Marseilles lay burning in the sun, one day."
city_name = sen[18:28]
output = len(city_name)❶ / len(sen)
print(output)
```

The output shows that we're nearly right:

```
0.16393442623
```

But we have calculated the **proportion**, but the exercise called for a **percentage**. We can easily fix this by multiplying by 100. Notice that the symbol for multiplication is not x, as you might think, but *. The final code:

---

1   Three, if you include just typing `city_name_length = 10`, but that would be rather boring!

```
from __future__ import division

sen = "Thirty years ago, Marseilles lay burning in the sun, one day."

# extract the city name and calculate the percentage
city_name = sen[18:28]
percentage = 100 * (len(city_name) / len(sen))

print(percentage)
```

place_name_2.py

gives the correct output:

```
16.393442623
```

although we probably don't really require that number of decimal places.

Place name, part three

The goal here is to capitalize **just** the place name and keep the rest of the sentence as it is. There are a couple of different ways of doing this, depending on how strict we want to be. One solution is to simply replace() the city name with an upper case version of itself:

```
sen = "Thirty years ago, Marseilles lay burning in the sun, one day."

city_name = sen[18:28]
upper_case_city_name = city_name.upper()
new_sentence = sen.replace(city_name, upper_case_city_name)

print(new_sentence)
```

In this code, we create two variables – upper_case_city_name and new_sentence – which are not really needed. If we want to be more concise we could write the same code like this:

```
sen = "Thirty years ago, Marseilles lay burning in the sun, one day."

city_name = sen[18:28]
print(sen.replace(city_name, city_name.upper()))
```

This version does the replacement and the printing all in a single line.

Just as before, however, we might want to think about a more flexible program. The solution above will work as long as there is only a single instance of the city name, but what if we are working with the whole book, and we want to replace just the first occurrence of the city name? In that situation, using the `replace()` method won't work, as it will replace all occurrences.

An alternative solution is to take advantage of the fact that we know the positions of the first and last characters in the city name. We can use these to split the text into three chunks – the bit before the city name, the city name itself, and the bit after. Then we just convert the city name to upper case and use + to stick the three bits back together:

```
sen = "Thirty years ago, Marseilles lay burning in the sun, one day."

# split the sentence into before, name and after
before_city_name = sen[0:18]
city_name = sen[18:28]
after_city_name = sen[28:]

# change the name to upper case and concatenate
print(before_city_name + city_name.upper() + after_city_name)
```

place_name_3.py

```
Thirty years ago, MARSEILLES lay burning in the sun, one day.
```

As the exercises in this book get longer, you'll notice that there are more and more different ways to write the code – you may end up with solutions that look very different to the example solutions. When trying to choose between different ways to write a program, always favour the solution that is clearest in intent and easiest to read.

What have we learned?

On the surface, these exercises are about manipulating pieces of text from Charles Dickens novels. It's very unlikely that you'll have to solve these exact same problems in your own programs!

On a deeper level, however, the exercises are about learning to break down problems into individual steps which can be solved using the tools available to us. Even the simplest of problems requires using several different tools in the right order. The remainder of the exercises in this book – and nearly all the programs you will write in the future – will require you to break down problems in this way.

We've also learned a few specific lessons. In the first exercise, we saw how it's important to test code using simple inputs in order to check that it's giving the right answer. In the swapping letters exercise, we saw that it can be challenging to keep track of the changes that are made to a variable as a program runs. In the last few exercises, we saw how different solutions to the same problem can have different levels of flexibility, and that it's a good idea to think about how a program will cope with a range of inputs.

We will return to these themes in future exercises.

3:   Reading and writing files

Why are we so interested in working with files?

Take a look back at the exercises from the end of the previous chapter. One of the things that they all have in common is that they involve working on **data** – in this case, text from books. The same is going to be true for the majority of the programs that you write, regardless of what types of problems you want to solve with Python. Whether you want to use Python for building web applications, creating games, or doing science, you'll be working with data of various types, and those data are going to be stored in files.

In the exercises from the previous chapter, we were given the data as part of the exercise description, and we included it directly in the program. Here's a reminder of the solution to the first exercise:

```
sentence = "It was the best of times, it was the worst of times, it was
the age of wisdom, it was the age of foolishness, it was the epoch of
belief, it was the epoch of incredulity, it was the season of Light, it
was the season of Darkness, it was the spring of hope, it was the winter
of despair, we had everything before us, we had nothing before us, we
were all going direct to Heaven, we were all going direct the other way
- in short, the period was so far like the present period, that some of
its noisiest authorities insisted on its being received, for good or for
evil, in the superlative degree of comparison only."

low_sentence = sentence.lower()

length = len(sentence)
a_count = low_sentence.count('a')
e_count = low_sentence.count('e')
i_count = low_sentence.count('i')
o_count = low_sentence.count('o')
u_count = low_sentence.count('u')
proportion = (a_count + e_count + i_count + o_count + u_count) / length

print("proportion of vowels is " + str(proportion))
```

Hopefully it's not too difficult to see the drawbacks of this approach. Even the bit of text above, which contains just over a hundred words, is awkward to include in a program – half of the program is devoted to just storing the text. Imagine doing the same thing with the complete text of *A Tale of Two Cities*, which is over a thousand times longer.

Including the data in the program in this way also makes the program inflexible. If we wanted to edit the above example to count the vowels in a different piece of text we'd have to open up the program in a text editor and copy & paste the new text in.

Storing the data in a separate file, and having our program read data from that file, will solve both these problems. With a separate data file, the program will just contain the code and it will be easier to understand. Also, if we want to change the data that the program operates on, we only have to change the data file, not the program itself.

Finally, using external data files will make it possible for us to tackle much more interesting problems and exercises and, as we'll see in the next chapter, will make it easier for us to explore Python's other features.

Reading text from a file

Firstly, a quick note about what we mean by text. In programming, when we talk about *text files*, we are not necessarily talking about something that is human readable. Rather, we are talking about a file that contains characters and lines – something that you could open up and view in a text editor, regardless of whether you could actually make sense of the file or not. Examples of text files which you might have encountered include:

- text from books, like in the exercises from the previous chapter

- files containing output from other programs

- documents that you have written, like emails or spreadsheets

- web pages

- and of course, Python code

In contrast, a lot of the files that you encounter day to day will be *binary files* – ones which are not made up of characters and lines, but of binary data. Examples include:

- image files which store photos and graphics (e.g. JPEGs and PNGs)

- audio files which store music (e.g. MP3 files)

- video files (there are many different formats!)

- compressed files (e.g. ZIP files)

If you're not sure whether a particular file is text or binary, there's a very simple way to tell – just open it up in a text editor. If the file displays without any problem, then it's text (regardless of whether you can make sense of it or not). If you get an error or a warning from your text editor, or the file displays as a collection of indecipherable characters, then it's binary.

The examples and exercises in this chapter are a little different from those in the previous one, because they rely on the existence of the files that we are going to manipulate. If you want to try running the examples in this chapter, you'll need to make sure that the file called *first_line.txt* is in your working folder. This file contains the opening sentence of *Little Dorrit*, and you'll find it in the *chapter_3* folder of the exercises download.

Using open() to read a file

In Python, as in the physical world, we have to open a file before we can read what's inside it. The Python function that carries out the job of opening a file is, very sensibly, called open(). It takes one argument – a string which contains the name of the file – and returns a *file object*:

```
my_file = open("first_line.txt")
```

A *file object* is a new data type which we haven't encountered before, and it's a little more complicated than the string and number types that we saw in the previous chapter. With strings and numbers it was easy to understand what they represented – a single bit of text, or a single number. A file object, in contrast, represents something a bit less tangible – it represents a file on your computer's hard drive.

The way that we use file objects is a bit different to strings and numbers as well. If you glance back at the examples from the previous chapter you'll see that most of the time when we want to use a variable containing a string or number we just use the variable name:

```
my_string = 'abcdefg'
print(my_string)
my_number = 42
print(my_number + 1)
```

In contrast, when we're working with file objects most of our interaction will be through *methods*. This style of programming will seem unusual at first, but as we'll see in this chapter, file objects have a well thought out set of methods which let us do lots of useful things.

The first thing we need to be able to do is to read the contents of the file. File objects have a `read()` method which does this. It doesn't take any arguments, and the return value is a string, which we can store in a variable. Once we've read the file contents into a variable, we can treat them just like any other string – for example, we can print them:

```
my_file = open("first_line.txt")
file_contents = my_file.read()
print(file_contents)
```

`print_file_contents.py`

Files, contents and file names

When learning to work with files it's very easy to get confused between a *file object*, a *file name*, and the *contents* of a file. Take a look at the following bit of code:

```
my_file_name = "first_line.txt"❶
my_file = open(my_file_name)❷
my_file_contents = my_file.read()❸
```

What's going on here? First we store the string "first_line.txt" in the variable my_file_name❶. Next, we use the variable my_file_name as

Chapter 3: Reading and writing files

the argument to the `open()` function, and store the resulting file object in the variable `my_file`❷. Finally, we call the `read()` method on the variable `my_file`, and store the resulting string in the variable `my_file_contents`❸.

The important thing to understand about this code is that there are three separate variables which have different types and which are storing three very different things:

- `my_file_name` is a string, and it stores the name of a file on disk.

- `my_file` is a file object, and it represents the file itself.

- `my_file_contents` is a string, and it stores the text that is in the file.

Remember from the previous chapter that variable names are **arbitrary** – the computer doesn't care what you call your variables. So this piece of code is exactly the same as the previous example:

```
apple = "first_line.txt"
banana = open(apple)
grape = banana.read()
```

except it is harder to understand! In contrast, the file name (*first_line.txt*) is **not** arbitrary – it **must** correspond to the name of a file on the hard drive of your computer, otherwise it will cause an error.

A very common error is to try to use the `read()` method on the wrong thing. Recall that `read()` is a method that only works on file objects. If we try to use the `read()` method on the file name:

```
my_file_name = "first_line.txt"
my_contents = my_file_name.read()
```

`read_error.py`

we'll get an `AttributeError` – Python will complain that strings don't have a `read()` method[1]:

```
AttributeError: 'str' object has no attribute 'read'
```

Another common error is to use the *file object* when we meant to use the *file contents*. If we try to print the file object:

```
my_file_name = "first_line.txt"
my_file = open(my_file_name)
print(my_file)
```

print_file_object.py

we won't get an error, but we'll get an odd looking line of output:

```
<open file 'first_line.txt', mode 'r' at 0x7fc5ff7784b0>
```

We won't discuss the meaning of this line now: just remember that if you try to print the contents of a file but instead you get some output that looks like the above, you have almost definitely printed the file **object** rather than the file **contents**.

Dealing with newlines

Let's take a look at the output we get when we try to print some information from a file. We'll use the *first_line.txt* file from the *chapter_3* examples folder. Remember, this file contains a single line with the first sentence of *Little Dorrit.* Open the file up in your text editor and take a look at it.

---

1   From now on, I'll just show the relevant bits of output when discussing error message.

We're going to write a simple program to read the sentence from the file and print it out along with its length. Putting together the file functions and methods from this chapter, and the material we saw in the previous chapter, we get the following code:

```
# open the file
my_file = open("first_line.txt")

# read the contents
sentence = my_file.read()

# calculate the length
length = len(sentence)

# print the output
print("sentence is " + sentence + " and length is " + str(length))
```

When we look at the output, we can see that there are two things wrong (as before, rather than show the whole output I've shortened it a bit):

```
sentence is Thirty years ago ... one day.
 and length is 62
```

Firstly, the output has been split over two lines, even though we didn't ask for it. And secondly, the length is wrong – there are only 61 characters in the sentence.

Both of these problems have the same explanation: Python has included the newline character at the end of the file as part of the contents. In other words, the variable sentence has a newline character at the end of it. If we could view the sentence variable directly[1], we would see that it looks like this:

---

1   In fact, we can do this – there's a function called repr() that returns a representation of a variable.

```
'Thirty years ago, Marseilles lay burning in the sun, one
day.\n'
```

This explains why the output from our program is split over two lines – the newline character is part of the string we are trying to print. It also explains why the length is wrong – Python is including the newline character when it counts the number of characters in the string.

The solution is simple. Because this is such a common problem, strings have a method for removing newline characters from the end of them. The method is called `rstrip()`, and it takes one string argument which is the character that you want to remove. In this case, we want to remove the newline character (\n). Here's a modified version of the code – note that the argument to `rstrip()` is itself a string so needs to be enclosed in quotes❶:

```
my_file = open("first_line.txt")
my_file_contents = my_file.read()

# remove the newline from the end of the file contents
sentence = my_file_contents.rstrip("\n")❶

length = len(sentence)
print("sentence is " + sentence + " and length is " + str(length))
```

print_sentence_and_length.py

and now the output looks just as we expected:

```
sentence is Thirty years ago ... one day. and length is 61
```

In the code above, we first read the file contents and then removed the newline, in two separate steps:

```
my_file_contents = my_file.read()
sentence = my_file_contents.rstrip("\n")
```

but it's more common to read the contents and remove the newline all in one go, like this:

```
sentence = my_file.read().rstrip("\n")
```

This is a bit tricky to read at first as we are using two different methods (read() and rstrip()) in the same statement. The key is to read it from left to right – we take the my_file variable and use the read() method on it, then we take the output of that method (which we know is a string) and use the rstrip() method on it. The result of the rstrip() method is then stored in the sentence variable.

If you find it difficult write the whole thing as one statement like this, just break it up and do the two things separately – your programs will run just as well.

Missing files

What happens if we try to read a file that doesn't exist?

```
my_file = open("nonexistent.txt")
```

We get a new type of error that we've not seen before:

```
IOError: [Errno 2] No such file or directory: 'nonexistent.txt'
```

If you encounter this error, you've probably got the file name wrong, or are working in the wrong folder.

Writing text to files

All the example programs that we've seen so far in this book have produced output straight to the screen. That's great for exploring new features and when working on programs, because it allows you us see the effect of changes to our code right away. It has a few drawbacks, however, when writing code that we might want to use in real life.

Printing output to the screen only really works well when there isn't very much of it[1]. It's great for short programs and status messages, but quickly becomes cumbersome for large amounts of output. Some terminals struggle with large amounts of text, or worse, have limited space which can cause the first bit of your output to disappear. It's not easy to search in output that's being displayed at the terminal, and long lines tend to get wrapped. Also, for many programs we want to send different bits of output to different files, rather than having it all dumped in the same place.

Most importantly, printed output vanishes when you close your terminal program or IDE. For small programs like the examples in this book, that's not a problem – if you want to see the output again you can just rerun the program. If you have a program that requires a few hours to run, that's not such a great option.

Opening files for writing

In the previous section, we saw how to open a file and read its contents. We can also open a file and *write* some data to it, but we have to use the open() function in a slightly different way. To open a file for writing, we use a two argument version of open(), where the second argument is a

---

1   Linux users may be aware that we can redirect terminal output to a file using shell redirection, which can get around some of these problems.

specially formatted string describing what we want to do to the file[1]. This second argument can be "r" for reading, "w" for writing, or "a" for appending[2]. If we leave out the second argument (like we did for all the examples above), Python uses the default, which is "r" for reading.

The difference between "w" and "a" is subtle, but important. If we open a file that already exists using the mode "w", then we will overwrite the current contents with whatever data we write to it. If we open an existing file with the mode "a", it will add new data onto the end of the file, but will **not** remove any existing content. If there doesn't already exist a file with the specified name, then "w" and "a" behave identically – they will both create a new file to hold the output.

Quite a lot of Python functions and methods have these optional arguments. For the purposes of this book, we will only mention them when they are directly relevant to what we're doing. If you want to see all the optional arguments for a particular method or function, the best place to look is the official Python documentation – we'll learn about this in chapter 8.

Once we've opened a file for writing, we can use the file `write()` method to write some text to it. `write()` works a lot like `print()` – it takes a single string argument – but instead of printing the string to the screen it writes it to the file.

Here's how we use `open()` with a second argument to open a file and write a single line of text to it:

```python
my_file = open("out.txt", "w")
my_file.write("Hello world")
```

write.py

---

1   We call this the *mode* of the file.
2   These are the most commonly used options – there are a few others.

Because the output is being written to the file in this example, you won't see any output on the screen if you run it. To check that the code has worked, you'll have to run it, then open up the file *out.txt* in your text editor and check that its contents are what you expect[1].

Remember that with `write()`, just like with `print()`, we can use **any** string as the argument. This also means that we can use any method or function that **returns** a string. The following are all perfectly OK:

```
# write "abcdef"
my_file.write("abc" + "def")

# write "6"
my_file.write(str(len('Hello')))

# write "Ho"
my_file.write("Hi".replace('i', 'o'))

# write "hello"
my_file.write("HELLO".lower())

# write contents of my_variable
my_file.write(my_variable)
```

Closing files

There's one more important file method to look at before we finish this chapter – `close()`. Unsurprisingly, this is the opposite of `open()` (but note that it's a *method*, whereas `open()` is a *function*). We should call `close()` after we're done reading or writing to a file – we won't go into the details here, but it's a good habit to get into as it avoids some types of bugs that can be tricky to track down[2]. `close()` is an unusual method as

---

1   .txt is the standard file name extension for a plain text file.
2   Specifically, it helps to ensure that output to a file is flushed, which is necessary when we want to make a file available to another program as part of our work flow.

it takes no arguments (so it's called with an empty pair of parentheses) and doesn't return any useful value:

```
my_file = open("out.txt", "w")
my_file.write("Hello world")
# remember to close the file
my_file.close()
```

close_file.py

Paths and folders

So far, we have only dealt with opening files in the same folder that we are running our program. What if we want to open a file from a different part of the file system?

The open() function is quite happy to deal with files from anywhere on your computer, as long as you give the full path (i.e. the sequence of folder names that tells you the location of the file). Just give the **path to the file** as the argument rather than the **name of the file**. The format of the file path looks different depending on your operating system. If you're using Windows, the path will look like this:

```
my_file = open("c:/windows/Desktop/myfolder/myfile.txt")
```

Notice that the folder names are separated by forward slashes rather than the back slashes that Windows normally uses. This is to avoid problems with special characters like the ones we saw in chapter 2.

If you're using a Mac or Linux machine, then the path will look slightly different:

```
my_file = open("/home/martin/myfolder/myfile.txt")
```

Getting user input

Sometimes we need to write a program that can get information from the user while it's running. For example, imagine we want to write a program that will print a customized greeting when you run it – the word 'Hello' followed by the user's name. One option is to put the name as a variable inside the program, then use string concatenation to print out the greeting:

```
name = "Martin"
print("Hello " + name)
```

This code is very easy to read, but it's not very convenient to use – if somebody else wants to run the program, then they have to edit the code and put their own name in the variable:

```
name = "Dave"
...
```

Another option is that we could use the file tools that we saw earlier to read the name from a file:

```
name = open("name.txt").read()
...
```

but this is still very inconvenient: the user has to create a new text file to just store their name. A better approach would be to have the program ask the user for their name when it runs. We can do this using the raw_input() function[1]. The raw_input() function takes a single

---

1   In Python 3, this function is simply called input().

string argument, which is a message to be displayed to the user, and returns whatever the user typed in as a string:

```
name = raw_input("What is your name?\n")
print("Hello " + name)
```

user_input.py

Notice that the message includes a newline character at the end so that the user can start typing on the next line.

Getting user input in this way can be very useful when we want to write a program that uses a file for input. We can ask the user for the name of the input file, then open and read the contents as we saw earlier:

```
file_name = raw_input("Enter the input file name\n")
input_file = open(file_name)
input_file_contents = input_file.read()
# do something with the file contents
```

This technique lets us choose the file that our program reads without having to edit the code.

Recap

We've taken a whole chapter to introduce the various ways of reading and writing to files, because it's such an important part of building programs that are useful in real life. We've seen how working with file contents is always a two step process – we must open a file before reading or writing – and looked at several common pitfalls.

We've also introduced a couple of new concepts that are more widely applicable. We've encountered our first example of an optional argument in the open() function (we'll see more of these in future chapters).

We've also encountered the first example of a complex data type – the file object – and seen how we can do useful things with it by calling its various methods, in contrast to the simple strings and numbers that we've been working with in the previous chapter. In future chapters, we'll learn about more of these complex data types and how to use them.

Exercises

Splitting a sentence

Look in the *chapter_3* exercises folder for a file called *curiosity_shop.txt* – it contains the same opening paragraph that we were using in the sentence lengths exercise from chapter 2. Write a program that will split the paragraph into two sentences and write each sentence to a separate file

Hint: use your solution to the sentence lengths exercise from chapter 2 as a starting point.

Writing a Comma Separated Value file

Comma Separated Value (usually called CSV for short) files are a simple way to store a table as plain text. The way it works is very simple: each row of the table becomes a line in the text file, and each column within a row is separated by a comma in the text file. For example, we could represent this table of birth and death years of authors:

Name	Born	Died
Charles Dickens	1812	1870
Jane Austen	1775	1817
Lewis Carroll	1832	1898

with a text file that looks like this:

```
Name, Born, Died
Charles Dickens, 1812, 1870
Jane Austen, 1775, 1817
Lewis Carroll, 1832, 1898
```

Here is a table showing details of three works by Charles Dickens:

Title	Completed	Type
The_Mudfog_Papers	1838	short stories
The Old Curiosity Shop	1841	NOVEL
A Christmas Carol	1843	novella

Notice that there is some odd formatting: the title of the first work has underscores instead of spaces, and the word NOVEL is in upper case. Write a program that will fix these formatting errors and create a CSV file to hold the information in the table.

Solutions

Splitting sentences

We have a head start on this problem, because we have already tackled a similar problem in the previous chapter. Let's remind ourselves of the solution we ended up with for that exercise:

```
text = "Night is generally ... any creature living."

period_position = text.find(".")
first_length = period_position + 1
second_length = len(text) - first_length
print("First sentence is " + str(first_length) + " characters long")
print("Second sentence is " + str(second_length) + " characters long")
```

What changes do we need to make? Firstly, we need to read the sentence from a file instead of writing it in the code:

```
text_file = open("curiosity_shop.txt")
text = text_file.read()
```

Secondly, instead of simply using the position of the period to figure out the lengths of the two sentences, we need to use it to actually extract the sentences from the text. We can do this using the substring notation that we learned about before. The first sentence goes from the start of the string (position zero) to the position after the period (since positions are exclusive at the end):

```
first_sentence = text[0:period_position+1]
```

and the second sentence goes from the first position after the period to the end of the text (remember that we can just leave off the second number to go all the way to the end):

```
second_sentence = text[period_position+1:]
```

Now that we have the two sentences stored in separate variables, we can tackle the problem of output. We need to open a new file to hold the first sentence, write the first sentence to the file, and then close it:

```
first_sentence_file = open("first_sentence.txt", "w")
first_sentence_file.write(first_sentence)
first_sentence_file.close()
```

and then do the same for the second sentence:

```
second_sentence_file = open("second_sentence.txt", "w")
second_sentence_file.write(second_sentence)
second_sentence_file.close()
```

If we put all these lines together, along with some spaces and comments to separate out the different bits of the program, we get this solution:

```
# open the input file and read the contents
text_file = open("curiosity_shop.txt")
text = text_file.read()

# find the position of the period which separates the sentences
period_position = text.find(".")

# extract the first sentence and write it to an output file
first_sentence = text[0:period_position+1]
first_sentence_file = open("first_sentence.txt", "w")
first_sentence_file.write(first_sentence)
first_sentence_file.close()

# extract the second sentence and write it to an output file
second_sentence = text[period_position+1:]
second_sentence_file = open("second_sentence.txt", "w")
second_sentence_file.write(second_sentence)
second_sentence_file.close()
```

splitting_sentences.py

Remember that this program won't produce any printed output; if you want to check that it's worked, you'll need to look at the contents of the two output files.

Writing a Comma Separated Value file

Let's start this problem by thinking about the variables we're going to need. We have three titles, three dates, and three types, so we'll need to use nine variables in all[1]:

---

1   If you're thinking at this point that this is a very inefficient way to to it, you're right! We'll see a better way in the next chapter.

```
title_1 = "The_Mudfog_Papers"
title_2 = "The Old Curiosity Shop"
title_3 = "A Christmas Carol"
date_1 = 1838
date_2 = 1841
date_3 = 1843
type_1 = "short stories"
type_2 = "NOVEL"
type_3 = "novella"
```

Let's ignore the formatting errors for now and just concentrate on the CSV output format. The first thing we need to do is open a file to write to:

```
csv_output = open("works.csv", "w")
```

Notice that we've called the output file *works.csv* rather than *works.txt*, to indicate that it has a particular format. Now we can start writing the lines of the CSV output. The first line gives the column headers:

```
csv_output.write("title, completed, type")
```

then for each of the three works we write the `title`, `date` and `type` variables separated by commas:

```
csv_output.write(title_1 + "," + date_1 + "," + type_1)
csv_output.write(title_2 + "," + date_2 + "," + type_2)
csv_output.write(title_3 + "," + date_3 + "," + type_3)
csv_output.close()
```

The logic here looks fine, but when we try to run this code we get an error:

```
  csv_output.write(title_1 + "," + date_1 + "," + type_1)
TypeError: cannot concatenate 'str' and 'int' objects
```

We have made the common mistake of mixing up strings and numbers. Look back at the piece of code where we defined the variables: the titles and types are stored as strings:

```
title_1 = "The_Mudfog_Papers"
type_1 = "short stories"
```

but the dates are stored as numbers:

```
date_1 = 1838
```

so in order to use the date in a concatenation, we need to use the `str()` function to turn it into a string:

```
csv_output.write(title_1 + "," + str(date_1) + "," + type_1)
csv_output.write(title_2 + "," + str(date_2) + "," + type_2)
csv_output.write(title_3 + "," + str(date_3) + "," + type_3)
```

Now the code runs, but when we look at the output it's not quite what we expected:

```
title, completed, typeThe_Mudfog_Papers,1838,short storiesThe
Old Curiosity Shop,1841,NOVELA Christmas Carol,1843,novella
```

All of the information we wanted is there, but rather than being split over separate lines, it's all jumbled together. This is because of a subtle different in the way that `write()` works compared to `print()`: with `write()`, if we want a newline character at the end of a line then we need to explicitly add it. Recall from chapter two that a newline character in Python is represented by "\n", so we just add that short string onto the end of each line that we write:

```
csv_output.write("title, completed, type\n")
csv_output.write(title_1 + "," + str(date_1) + "," + type_1 + "\n")
csv_output.write(title_2 + "," + str(date_2) + "," + type_2 + "\n")
csv_output.write(title_3 + "," + str(date_3) + "," + type_3 + "\n")
```

Now the output has the structure we want:

```
title, completed, type
The_Mudfog_Papers,1838,short stories
The Old Curiosity Shop,1841,NOVEL
A Christmas Carol,1843,novella
```

On to the last bit of the exercise: fixing the formatting errors. For the title, we can use `replace()` to substitute the underscores with spaces:

```
new_title_1 = title_1.replace('_', ' ')
```

For the upper case type, we can use the `lower()` method to turn it back into lower case:

```
new_type_2 = type_2.lower()
```

We have to remember to change the variable names in the `write()` statements as well. Here's the final version:

```
# store all the titles, dates and types
title_1 = "The_Mudfog_Papers"
title_2 = "The Old Curiosity Shop"
title_3 = "A Christmas Carol"
date_1 = 1838
date_2 = 1841
date_3 = 1843
type_1 = "short stories"
type_2 = "NOVEL"
type_3 = "novella"

# fix the formatting errors
new_title_1 = title_1.replace('_', ' ')
new_type_2 = type_2.lower()

# open the output file and write the output
csv_output = open("works.csv", "w")
csv_output.write("title, completed, type\n")
csv_output.write(new_title_1 + "," + str(date_1) + "," + type_1 + "\n")
csv_output.write(title_2 + "," + str(date_2) + "," + new_type_2 + "\n")
csv_output.write(title_3 + "," + str(date_3) + "," + type_3 + "\n")
csv_output.close()
```

writing_csv.py

If you try running this program yourself, remember that it won't produce any output on the screen – all of the output is written to the CSV file, so you won't see anything when you run it. In order to check that it's worked, you'll need to open the *works.csv* file in a text editor (or in a spreadsheet program).

Looking at the solution we came up with, it seems like there's a lot of redundancy there. We start the program by creating a bunch of variables with very similar names, and then later on, we have three nearly identical statements which use the write() method. Although the solution works, it seems to involve a lot of unnecessary typing! Also, having so much nearly identical code seems likely to cause errors if we need to change something. In the next chapter, we'll examine some tools which will allow us to start removing some of that redundancy.

What have we learned?

The exercises for this chapter have been about the simple mechanics of reading and writing files. The majority of programs that you'll want to write will involve files in some capacity, so exercises like these are good practice.

We've also encountered a few specific problems that are commonly encountered when working with files. We've seen how easy it is to accidentally forget the difference between strings and numbers, and how we can fix the error by converting values from one type to another. We've also seen the difference between `print()` and `write()` in the way that they handle line endings.

4: Lists and loops

Why do we need lists and loops?

Think back over the exercises that we've seen in the previous two chapters – they've all involved dealing with one bit of information at a time. In chapter 2, we used string manipulation tools to process single sentences, and in chapter 3, we practised reading and writing files one at a time. The closest we got to using multiple pieces of data was during the final exercise in chapter 3, where we were dealing with information for three different works.

If you think for a moment about the types of problems that you want to solve and the things you want to build using Python, you'll quickly see that we're going to need to be able to deal with multiple pieces of data all the time. If we're writing a game, we might have to keep track of multiple players; if we're building a blogging tool then we need to manage multiple posts. Even if we just want to build a simple to-do list app, we'll need to store a collection of tasks. In this chapter, we'll learn about the fundamental programming tools that will allow our programs to do these things.

So far we have learned about several different data types (strings, numbers, and file objects), all of which store a single bit of information[1]. When we've needed to store multiple bits of information (for example, the three book titles in the chapter 3 exercises) we have simply created more variables to hold them:

---

[1] We know that files are slightly different to strings and numbers because they can store a lot of information, but each file object still only refers to a single file.

```
title_1 = "The_Mudfog_Papers"
title_2 = "The Old Curiosity Shop"
title_3 = "A Christmas Carol"
```

The limitations of this approach became clear quite quickly as we looked at the solution code – it only worked because the number of books was small, and we knew the number in advance. If we were to repeat the exercise with three hundred or three thousand books, then the vast majority of the code would be given over to storing variables and it would become completely unmanageable. And if we were to try and write a program that could process an unknown number of books (for instance, by reading them from a file), we wouldn't be able to do it, because we wouldn't know in advance how many variables to create. To make our programs able to process multiple pieces of data, we need an entirely new type of structure which can hold many pieces of information at the same time – a *list*.

We've also dealt exclusively with programs whose statements are executed from top to bottom in a very straightforward way. This has great advantages when first starting to think about programming – it makes it very easy to follow the flow of a program. The downside of this sequential style of programming, however, is that it leads to very redundant code like we saw at the end of the previous chapter:

```
csv_output.write(new_title_1 + "," + str(date_1) + "," + type_1 + "\n")
csv_output.write(title_2 + "," + str(date_2) + "," + new_type_2 + "\n")
csv_output.write(title_3 + "," + str(date_3) + "," + type_3 + "\n")
```

Again; it was only possible to solve the exercise in this manner because we knew in advance the number of lines of output we were going to need. Looking at the code, it's clear that these three statements consist of essentially the same statement being executed multiple times, with some slight variations. This idea of repetition with variation is incredibly common in programming problems, and Python has a built in tool for expressing it – *loops*.

Creating lists and retrieving elements

To make a new list, we put several strings or numbers[1] inside square brackets, separated by commas:

```
authors = ["Charles Dickens", "Jane Austen", "Lewis Carroll"]
ages_at_death = [58, 41, 65]
```

Each individual item in a list is called an *element*. To get a single element from the list, write the variable name followed by the *index* of the element you want in square brackets:

```
authors = ["Charles Dickens", "Jane Austen", "Lewis Carroll"]

print(authors[1])
first_author = authors[0]
print(first_author)
```

create_list.py

If we want to go in the other direction – i.e. we know which element we want but we don't know the index – we can use the index() method, which takes an argument of any type and returns the position of the argument in the list:

```
authors = ["Charles Dickens", "Jane Austen", "Lewis Carroll"]
jane_index = authors.index("Jane Austen")
# jane_index is now 1
```

---

1   Or in fact, any other type of value or variable

Remember that in Python we start counting from zero rather than one, so the first element of a list is always at index zero. If we give a negative number, Python starts counting from the **end** of the list rather than the beginning – so it's easy to get the last element from a list:

```
last_author = authors[-1]
```

What if we want to get more than one element from a list? We can give a start and stop position, separated by a colon, to specify a range of elements:

```
books = ["Oliver Twist", "Bleak House", "Hard Times", "Little Dorrit"]
early_books = books[0:2]
# early books are Oliver Twist and Bleak House
```

sublist.py

Does this look familiar? It's the exact same notation that we used to get substrings back in chapter 2, and it works in exactly the same way – numbers are **inclusive** at the start and **exclusive** at the end. The fact that we use the same notation for strings and lists hints at a deeper relationship between the two types. In fact, what we were doing when extracting substrings in chapter 2 was **treating a string as though it were a list of characters**. This idea – that we can treat a variable as though it were a list when it's not – is a powerful one in Python and we'll come back to it later in this chapter.

Working with list elements

To add another element onto the end of an existing list, we can use the append() method:

```
characters = ["Pip", "Joe", "Estella"]
print(characters)
characters.append("Miss Havisham")
print(characters)
```

append.py

append() is an interesting method because it actually changes the variable on which it's used – in the above example, the characters list goes from having three elements to having four:

```
['Pip', 'Joe', 'Estella']
['Pip', 'Joe', 'Estella', 'Miss Havisham']
```

We can get the length of a list by using the len() function, just like we did for strings:

```
characters = ["Pip", "Joe", "Estella"]
print("There are " + str(len(characters)) + " characters")
characters.append("Miss Havisham")
print("Now there are " + str(len(characters)) + " characters")
```

list_length.py

The output shows that the number of elements in characters really has changed:

```
There are 3 characters
Now there are 4 characters
```

We can concatenate two lists just as we did with strings, by using the plus symbol:

```
male_characters = ["Pip", "Joe", "Magwitch"]
female_characters = ["Estella", "Miss Havisham"]
all_characters = male_characters + female_characters

print(str(len(male_characters)) + " male characters")
print(str(len(female_characters)) + " female characters")
print(str(len(all_characters)) + " total characters")
```

concatenate_lists.py

As we can see from the output, this doesn't change either of the two original lists – it makes a brand new list which contains elements from both:

```
3 male characters
2 female characters
5 total characters
```

If we want to add elements from a list onto the end of an existing list, changing it in the process, we can use the extend() method. extend() behaves like append() but takes a *list* as its argument rather than a single *element*:

```
male_characters = ["Pip", "Joe", "Magwitch"]
male_characters.extend(["Matthew", "Herbert"])
# now male_characters has five elements
```

Here are two more list methods that change the variable they're used on: reverse() and sort(). Both reverse() and sort() work by changing the order of the elements in the list. If we want to print out a list to see how this works, we need to used str() just as we did when printing out numbers:

```
characters = ["Pip", "Joe", "Magwitch", "Estella"]
print("at the start : " + str(characters))

characters.reverse()
print("after reversing : " + str(characters))

characters.sort()
print("after sorting : " + str(characters))
```

reverse_and_sort.py

If we take a look at the output, we can see how the order of the elements in the list is changed by these two methods:

```
at the start : ['Pip', 'Joe', 'Magwitch', 'Estella'
after reversing : ['Estella', 'Magwitch', 'Joe', 'Pip']
after sorting : ['Estella', 'Joe', 'Magwitch', 'Pip']
```

By default, Python sorts strings in alphabetical order and numbers in ascending numerical order[1].

Writing a loop

Imagine we wanted to take our list of characters from *Great Expectations*:

```
characters = ["Pip", "Joe", "Magwitch", "Estella"]
```

and print out each element on a separate line, like this:

```
Pip is a character from Great Expectations
Joe is a character from Great Expectations
Magwitch is a character from Great Expectations
Estella is a character from Great Expectations
```

One way to do it would be to just print each element separately:

---

1   We can sort in other ways too, but it requires a few concepts that we've not covered yet so we
     won't discuss it here.

```
print(characters[0] + " is a character from Great Expectations")
print(characters[1] + " is a character from Great Expectations")
print(characters[2] + " is a character from Great Expectations")
print(characters[3] + " is a character from Great Expectations")
```

but this is very repetitive and relies on us knowing the number of elements in the list. What we need is a way to say something along the lines of "*for each element in the list of characters, print out the element, followed by the words ' is a character from Great Expectations'*". Python's loop syntax allows us to express those instructions like this:

```
characters = ["Pip", "Joe", "Magwitch", "Estella"]
for character in characters:
    print(character + " is a character from Great Expectations")
```

loop.py

Let's take a moment to look at the different parts of this loop. We start by writing for x in y, where y is the name of the list we want to process and x is the name we want to use for the current element each time round the loop.

x is just a variable name (so it follows all the rules that we've already learned about variable names), but it behaves slightly differently to all the other variables we've seen so far. In all previous examples, we create a variable and store something in it, and then the value of that variable doesn't change unless we change it ourselves. In contrast, when we create a variable to be used in a loop, we don't set its value – the value of the variable will be automatically set to each element of the list in turn, and it will be different each time round the loop.

This first line of the loop ends with a colon, and all the subsequent lines (just one, in this case) are indented. Indented lines can start with any number of tab or space characters, but they must all be indented in the same way. This pattern – a line which ends with a colon, followed by some indented lines – is very common in Python, and we'll see it in several more places throughout this book. A group of indented lines is often called a *block* of code[1].

In this case, we refer to the indented block as the *body* of the loop, and the lines inside it will be executed once for each element in the list. To refer to the current element, we use the variable name that we wrote in the first line. The body of the loop can contain as many lines as we like, and can include all the functions and methods that we've learned about, with one important exception: we're not allowed to change the list while inside the body of the loop[2].

Here's an example of a loop with a more complicated body:

```
characters = ["Pip", "Joe", "Magwitch"]
for character in characters:
    name_length = len(character)
    first_letter = character[0]
    print(character + " is a character from Great Expectations")
    print("His name starts with " + first_letter)
    print("His name has " + str(name_length) + " letters")
```

complex_loop.py

The body of the loop in the code above has five statements, three of which are `print()` statements, so each time round the loop we'll get three lines of output. Because the list contains three elements, the loop will be run three times, for a total of nine lines of output as we can see:

---

1   If you're familiar with any other programming languages, you might know code blocks as things that are surrounded with curly brackets – the indentation does the same job in Python.

2   Changing the list while looping can cause Python to become confused about which elements have already been processed and which are yet to come.

```
Pip is a character from Great Expectations
His name starts with P
His name has 3 letters
Joe is a character from Great Expectations
His name starts with J
His name has 3 letters
Magwitch is a character from Great Expectations
His name starts with M
His name has 8 letters
```

Why is the above approach better than printing out these nine lines in nine separate statements? Well, for one thing, there's much less redundancy – here we only needed to write three `print()` statements. This also means that if we need to make a change to the code, we only have to make it once rather than three separate times. Another benefit of using a loop here is that if we want to add some elements to the list, we don't have to touch the loop code at all. Consequently, it doesn't matter how many elements are in the list, and it's not a problem if we don't know the size of the list when we write the code.

Indentation errors

Unfortunately, introducing tools like loops that require an indented block of code also introduces the possibility of a new type of error – an `IndentationError`. Notice what happens when the indentation of one of the lines in the block does not match the others ❶:

```
characters = ["Pip", "Joe", "Magwitch"]
for character in characters:
    name_length = len(character)
 ❶first_letter = character[0]
    print(character + " is a character from Great Expectations")
    print("His name starts with " + first_letter)
    print("His name has " + str(name_length) + " letters")
```

When we run this code, we get an error message before the program even starts to run:

```
IndentationError: unindent does not match any outer indentation level
```

When you encounter an `IndentationError`, go back to your code and double check that all the lines in the block match up. Also double check that you are using either tabs or spaces for indentation, **not both**. The easiest way to do this, as mentioned in chapter 1, is to enable *tab emulation* in your text editor or IDE.

Using a string as a list

We've already seen how a string can pretend to be a list – we can use list index notation to get individual characters or substrings from inside a string. Can we also use loop notation to process a string as though it were a list? Yes – if we write a loop statement with a string in the position where we'd normally find a list, Python treats **each character** in the string as a separate element. This allows us to very easily process a string one letter at a time:

```python
name = "Magwitch"
for letter in name:
    print("one letter is " + letter)
```

string_as_list.py

In this case, we're just printing each individual character:

```
one letter is M
one letter is a
one letter is g
one letter is w
one letter is I
one letter is t
one letter is c
one letter is h
```

This is a useful feature, but it can also sometimes be annoying – if you write a loop and expect to see multiple lines of output, but instead see only single letters, then you've probably put a **string** in the for line where you should have put a **list**.

The process of repeating a set of instructions for each element of a list (or character in a string) is called *iteration*, and we often talk about *iterating over* a list or string.

Splitting a string to make a list

So far in this chapter, all our lists have been written manually. However, there are plenty of functions and methods in Python that produce lists as their output. One such method that is particularly interesting when we're working with text is the split() method which works on strings. split() takes a single argument, called the *delimiter*, and splits the original string wherever it sees the delimiter, producing a list. Here's an example which takes a sentence and splits it into words:

```
sen = "Thirty years ago, Marseilles lay burning in the sun, one day."
words = sen.split(" ")
print(words)
```

split.py

We can see from the output that the string has been split wherever there was a space, leaving us with a list of words:

```
['Thirty', 'years', 'ago,', 'Marseilles', 'lay', 'burning', 'in', 'the',
'sun,', 'one', 'day.']
```

Of course, once we've created a list in this way we can iterate over it using a loop, just like any other list.

Iterating over lines in a file

Another very useful thing that we can iterate over is a **file object**. Just as a string can pretend to be a list for the purposes of looping, a file object can do the same trick. When we treat a **string** as a list, each character becomes an individual element, but when we treat a **file** as a list, each **line** becomes an individual element. This makes processing a file line by line very easy:

```
file = open("some_input.txt")
for line in file:
    # do something with the line
```

Notice that in this example we are iterating over the file object, **not** over the file contents. If we iterate over the file contents like this:

```
file = open("some_input.txt")
contents = file.read()
for line in contents:
    # warning: line contains just a single character!
```

then each time round the loop we will be dealing with a single character, which is probably not what we want. A good way to avoid this mistake is to ask yourself, whenever you open a file, whether you want to get the contents as one big string (in which case you should use `read()`) or line by line (in which case you should iterate over the file object).

Another common pitfall is to iterate over the same file object twice:

```
file = open("some_input.txt")

# print the length of each line
for line in file:
    print("The length is " + str(len(line)))

# print the first character of each line
for line in file:
    print("The first character is " + line[0])
```

If we run this code, we'll find that the second `for` loop never gets executed. The reason for this is that file objects are **exhaustible**. Once we have iterated over a file object, Python "remembers" that it is already at the end of the file, so when we try to iterate over it again, there are no lines remaining to be read. One way round this problem is to close and reopen the file each time we want to iterate over it:

```
# print the length of each line
file = open("some_input.txt")
for line in file:
    print("The length is " + str(len(line)))
file.close()

# print the first character of each line
file = open("some_input.txt")
for line in file:
    print("The first character is " + line[0])
file.close()
```

A better approach is to read the lines of the file into a list, then iterate over the list (which we can safely do multiple times). The file object `readlines()` method returns a list of all the lines in a file, and we can use it like this:

```
# first store a list of lines in the file
file = open("some_input.txt")
all_lines = file.readlines()

# print the lengths
for line in all_lines:
    print("The length is " + str(len(line)))

# print the first characters
for line in all_lines:
    print("The first character is " + line[0])
```

readlines.py

Looping with ranges

Sometimes we want to loop over a list of numbers. Imagine we have a string:

```
name = "Estella"
```

and we want to print out the first letter, then the first two letters, then the first three letters, etc. like this:

```
E
Es
Est
Este
Estel
Estell
Estella
```

We can use the substring notation that we learned in chapter 2 to extract the bit of the name we want to print. If we try writing it without a loop, then we get very repetitive code:

```
print(name[0:1])
print(name[0:2])
print(name[0:3])
...
```

Looking at this code, the structure of the problem becomes clear: each time we print out a line, the end position of the substring needs to increase by one. Obviously we need a loop to do this, but what are we going to iterate over? We can't just iterate over the name string itself, because that will give us individual letters, which is not what we want. We can manually assemble a list of end positions, and loop over that:

```
stop_positions = [1,2,3,4,5,6,7]
for stop in stop_positions:
    substring = name[0:stop]
    print(substring)
```

but this seems cumbersome, and only works if we know the length of the name in advance.

A better solution is to use the range() function. range() is a built in Python function that generates lists of numbers for us to loop over. The behaviour of range() depends on how many arguments we give it. Below are a few examples, with the output following directly after the code.

With a single argument, range() will count up from zero to that number, excluding the number itself:

```
for number in range(6):
    print(number)
```

```
0
1
2
3
4
5
```

With two numbers, range() will count up from the first number (inclusive[1]) to the second (exclusive):

```
for number in range(3, 8):
    print(number)
```

```
3
4
5
6
7
```

With three numbers, range() will count up from the first to the second with the step size given by the third:

```
for number in range(2, 14, 4):
    print(number)
```

```
2
6
10
```

---

1   The rules for ranges are the same as for array notation – inclusive on the low end, exclusive on the high end – so you only have to memorize them once!

Knowing how to use the `range()` function, we can rewrite our code from before to generate the list of stop positions automatically:

```
name = "Estella"
for stop in range(1,len(name) + 1):
    substring = name[0:stop]
    print(substring)
```

name_range.py

Notice how this version of the code will work for any name of any length.

Recap

In this chapter we've seen several tools that work together to allow our programs to deal elegantly with multiple pieces of data. Lists let us store many elements in a single variable, and loops let us process those elements one by one. In learning about loops, we've also been introduced to the block syntax and the importance of indentation in Python.

We've also seen several useful ways in which we can use the notation we've learned for working with lists with other types of data. Depending on the circumstances, we can use *strings*, *files*, and *ranges* as if they were lists. This is a very helpful feature of Python, because once we've become familiar with the syntax for working with lists, we can use it in many different place. Learning about these tools has also helped us make sense of some interesting behaviour that we observed in earlier chapters.

Lists are the first example we've encountered of structures that can hold multiple pieces of data. We'll encounter another such structure – the *dict* – in chapter 7.

Exercises

Note: all the files mentioned in these exercises can be found in the *chapter_4* folder of the files download.

Processing lines in a file

The file *two_cities.txt* contains the first bit of the opening sentence of *A Tale of Two Cities*, split up over multiple lines like this:

```
it was the best of times
it was the worst of times
it was the age of wisdom
it was the age of foolishness
it was the epoch of belief
it was the epoch of incredulity
it was the season of Light
it was the season of Darkness
it was the spring of hope
it was the winter of despair
```

There are a total of ten lines. Each line begins with the exact same phrase: "it was the". Write a program that will remove this phrase from the start of each line and write the remainder to a new file. The first few lines of the new file should read:

```
best of times
worst of times
...
```

Your program should also print the length of each trimmed line to the screen as it's running.

Extracting speech from text

The file *great_expectations.txt* contains a passage from near the beginning of *Great Expectations*. If we open it up in a text editor we'll see that it contains quite a bit of dialogue, mixed in with descriptive text:

```
I was soon at the Battery ... I opened the bundle and emptied my
pockets.

"What's in the bottle, boy?" said he.

"Brandy," said I.

He was already handing ... without biting it off.

"I think you have got the ague," said I.

"I'm much of your opinion, boy," said he.

"It's bad about here," I told him. "You've been lying out on the
meshes, and they're dreadful aguish. Rheumatic too."
```

The file *speech.txt* contains the start and stop positions of all the spoken sections of the text. If we look at the first few lines of this file:

```
622,650
661,670
1058,1090
```

it tells us that there is a section of dialogue between characters 622 and 650, then another section between characters 661 and 670, and so on. There are around 30 spoken lines in the passage, so there are a total of 30 lines in this file.

Write a program that will use the start and stop positions in the *speech.txt* file to extract **just** the spoken words from the *great_expectations.txt* file and write them to a new file. Every line of the new file will contain a single spoken section, so the first few lines will look like this:

```
"What's in the bottle, boy?"
"Brandy,"
"I think you have got the ague,"
"I'm much of your opinion, boy,"
```

Hint: you'll be dealing with two input files – for each one, think about whether you want to read the contents as one big string, or whether you want to process the file one line at a time.

Solutions

Processing lines in a file

This seems a bit more complicated than previous exercises – we are being asked to write a program that does two things at once! – so lets tackle it one step at a time. First, we'll write a program that simply reads each line from the file and prints it to the screen:

```
file = open("two_cities.txt")
for line in file:
    print(line)
```

We can see from the output that we've forgotten to remove the newline character from the ends of the lines, so there is a blank line between each:

```
it was the best of times

it was the worst of times

it was the age of wisdom

...
```

but we'll ignore that for now. The next step is to remove the first bit of each line, and there are two different approaches we can take. One is to simply count the number of characters that we want to remove (it turns out to be 11 characters, remembering to include space) and use a substring to get the part of the line after "it was the ".

Here's what the code looks like with the substring part added:

```
file = open("two_cities.txt")
for line in file:
    trimmed_line = line[11:]
    print(trimmed_line)
```

As before, we are simply printing the trimmed lines to the screen, and from the output we can confirm that the phrase has been removed from each line:

```
best of times

worst of times

age of wisdom

...
```

Now that we know our code is working, we'll switch from printing to the screen to writing to a file. Whenever we're writing text to a file using a loop, we have to be very careful about where we open and close the file. We have to open the file **before** the loop❶, then write the trimmed lines to the file **inside** the loop❷, then close the file **after** the loop❸:

```
file = open("two_cities.txt")
output = open("trimmed.txt", "w")❶

for line in file:
    trimmed_line = line[11:]
    output.write(trimmed_line)❷

output.close()❸
```

If we open the output file **inside** the loop like this❶ :

```
file = open("two_cities.txt")
for line in file:
    output = open("trimmed.txt", "w")  ❶
    trimmed_line = line[11:]
    output.write(trimmed_line)

output.close()
```

then the output file will get overwritten each time round the loop and we'll end up with only the final line.

On the other hand, if we close the file inside the loop like this❶ :

```
file = open("two_cities.txt")
output = open("trimmed.txt", "w")

for line in file:
    trimmed_line = line[11:]
    output.write(trimmed_line)
    output.close()❶
```

then the second time round the loop the file will already be closed and we'll get an error when we try to write to it.

Opening up the *trimmed.txt* file, we can see that the result looks good. It didn't matter that we never removed the newlines, because they appear in the correct place in the output file anyway:

```
best of times
worst of times
age of wisdom
age of foolishness
epoch of belief
epoch of incredulity
season of Light
season of Darkness
spring of hope
winter of despair
```

Now the final step – printing the lengths to the screen – requires just one more line of code. Here's the final program in full, with comments:

```
# open the input file
file = open("two_cities.txt")

# open the output file
output = open("trimmed.txt", "w")

# process each line in turn
for line in file:
    # trim the line and add it to the output file
    trimmed_line = line[11:]
    output.write(trimmed_line)

    # print a message to the screen
    print("wrote a line with " + str(len(trimmed_line)) + " characters")

output.close()
```

trim_lines.py

Extracting speech from text

This is a similar exercise to the place name exercise from chapter 2. In that exercise, we were given a start position and a stop position and asked to write a program that would extract the text between those two positions. This exercise has two important differences. Firstly, there are multiple start/stop positions rather than just one. Secondly, rather than being given the start/stop positions as part of the exercise description we have to read them from a file.

Let's concentrate on the new bit of the problem first – reading the file of start/stop positions. As before, we can start by opening up the file:

```
speech_locations = open("speech.txt")
```

Before we can decide on the next step, we have to think about how we want to process this file – do we want the whole file, or do we want it line by line? Given that each pair of positions is on a separate line, it makes sense to deal with them individually, so we will use a `for` loop to process the file one line (i.e. one bit of speech) at a time:

```
for line in speech_locations:
    print(line)
```

The above code gives us a loop that allows us to process one line at a time. For now, it doesn't do anything interesting with the line, it just prints it:

```
622,650

661,670

1058,1090

1100,1132

...
```

If we look at the output, we can see that we still have a newline at the end of each line, but we'll not worry about that for now.

Next, we have to split up each line into a start and stop position. The `split()` method is probably a good choice for this job – let's see what happens when we split each line using a comma as the delimiter:

```
for line in speech_locations:
    split_line = line.split(',')
    print(split_line)
```

The output shows that each line, when split, turns into a list of two elements:

```
['622', '650\n']
['661', '670\n']
['1058', '1090\n']
...
```

Notice that the second element of each list has a newline on the end, because we haven't removed them.

In each list, the first element is the start position and the second element is the stop position. We can use square brackets to get the first❶ and second❷ elements individually, store them in variables, and print the variables:

```
for line in speech_locations:
    split_line = line.split(',')
    start = split_line[0]❶
    stop = split_line[1]❷
    print("start is " + start + ", stop is " + stop)
```

The output shows that this approach works – the `start` and `stop` variables take different values each time round the loop:

```
start is 622, stop is 650
start is 661, stop is 670
start is 1058, stop is 1090
...
```

Now we have a way of storing the start and stop positions in variables, we can try using them to extract the relevant bits of the text. In order to get hold of the text, we need to open the *great_expectations.txt* file:

```
text = open("great_expectations.txt")
```

and then, just as before, decide what to do with it. For this file, we **don't** want to process it line by line; instead we want to get the entire contents as one big string, so we use the read() method:

```
text = open("great_expectations.txt").read()
```

Now we can put these two bits of information – the text, and the start/stop positions – together to extract the speech. For now, we'll just print the extracted bits of text to the screen so that we can see if the program works:

```
text = open("great_expectations.txt").read()
speech_locations = open("speech.txt")

for line in speech_locations:
    split_line = line.split(',')
    start = split_line[0]
    stop = split_line[1]
    speech = text[start:stop]❶
    print(speech)
```

Unfortunately, when we run this code we get an error at the point where we use the start and stop positions❶:

```
TypeError: slice indices must be integers or None or have an __index__
method
```

What has gone wrong? Remember that when we use split() on a string the result is a **list of strings**. This means that the start and stop variables in our program are also strings (because they're just individual elements of the split_line list). The problem comes when we try to use them as numbers. Fortunately, it's easily fixed – we just have to use the int() function to turn our strings into numbers:

```
start = int(split_line[0])
stop = int(split_line[1])
```

and the program works as intended and prints out just the extracted bits
of the text:

```
"What's in the bottle, boy?"
"Brandy,"
"I think you have got the ague,"
"I'm much of your opinion, boy,"
"It's bad about here,"
...
```

Now on to the final step: instead of just printing the speech we want to
write it to a file. The code for this bit will be very similar to the first
exercise: we need to open a file **before** the loop, write the lines **inside** the
loop, and close the file **outside** the loop. Here's the final version with
comments – note that we end each line of output with a newline
character to make sure that each bit of dialogue is on a separate line:

```
# open the file which contains the whole text and read the contents
text = open("great_expectations.txt").read()

# open the file which contains the speech locations
speech_locations = open("speech.txt")

# open the output file where we want to save the dialogue
output = open("extracted_speech.txt", "w")

# process the speech locations one line at a time
for line in speech_locations:
    # get the start and stop positions as numbers
    split_line = line.split(',')
    start = int(split_line[0])
    stop = int(split_line[1])

    # extract the text and write it to the output file
    speech = text[start:stop]
    output.write(speech + "\n")

output.close()
```

extract_speech.py

This is the most complicated code we've written so far, so take a moment to read through and make sure that you understand what's going on. Remember that there are three files involved in this program – the text, the speech locations, and the output file.

What have we learned?

Unless you often work with text analysis and data mining, this might not seem like a very realistic exercise. However, if we forget for a moment about the specifics and think about the general theme of the problem – bringing together data from two different sources, processing them, and saving the result – it should be clear that many different programming problems fall into this category.

We'll see many more examples of lists and loops in the remainder of this book, and have plenty more opportunities to practice using them in the exercises. However, these exercises have illustrated a few important points. We've seen how switching between printing and writing output can be a useful strategy when working on code and how, when using loops and files together, we have to be particularly careful of the order in which we do things. The second exercise gave us an insight into the problems associated with splitting up files into chunks of data – particularly when we want to treat some of the data as numbers.

5: Writing our own functions

Why do we want to write our own functions?

Take a look back at the very first exercise in this book – the one in chapter 2 where we had to write a program to calculate the proportion of vowels in a piece of text. Let's remind ourselves of the code:

```
text = "It was the ... comparison only."
low_text = text.lower()
length = len(text)
a_count = low_text .count('a')
e_count = low_text .count('e')
i_count = low_text .count('i')
o_count = low_text .count('o')
u_count = low_text .count('u')
proportion = (a_count + e_count + i_count + o_count + u_count) / length
print("proportion of vowels is " + str(proportion))
```

If we discount the first line (whose job is to store the input string) and the last line (whose job is to print the result), we can see that it takes eight lines of code to calculate the proportion of vowels. If we're prepared to make the individual statements a bit more complicated by doing lower() and count() in the same statement, we can remove a couple of lines:

```
text = "It was the ... comparison only."
a_count = text.lower().count('a')
e_count = text.lower().count('e')
i_count = text.lower().count('i')
o_count = text.lower().count('o')
u_count = text.lower().count('u')
prop = (a_count + e_count + i_count + o_count + u_count) / len(text)
print("proportion of vowels is " + str(prop))
```

but we are still left with six lines of calculation. This means that every place in our code where we want to calculate the number of vowels in a piece of text, we need these same six lines – and we have to make sure we copy them exactly, without any mistakes.

It would be much simpler if Python had a built in function (let's call it `get_vowel_prop()`) for calculating proportion of vowels. If that were the case, then we could just run `get_vowel_prop()` in the same way we run `print()`, or `len()`, or `open()`. Although, sadly, Python does not have such a built in function, it does have the next best thing – a way for us to create our own functions.

There are some obvious benefits to creating our own function to carry out a particular job. For example, it allows us to reuse the same code many times within a program without having to copy it out each time. We can even reuse code across multiple different programs.

Putting code into functions has other benefits that are not so obvious. Functions allow us to split up our code into logical units, which makes it possible to work on different bits of the code independently. This kind of logical separation is what makes it possible to work on very large programs without getting confused. In this chapter, we'll take a look at the basics of writing functions and see how to make them useful and flexible. At the end of the chapter, we'll also talk about how to write functions in a way that maximises your ability to deal with complex problems.

Defining a function

Let's go ahead and create our `get_vowel_prop()` function. Before we start typing, we need to figure out what the inputs (the number and types of the *function arguments*) and outputs (the type of the *return value*) are going to be. For this function, that seems pretty obvious – the input is going to be a single text string, and the output is going to be a decimal number. To translate these into Python terms: the function will take a single argument of type *string*, and will return a value of type *number*[1]. Here's the code:

```python
def get_vowel_prop(text):
    a_count = text.lower().count('a')
    e_count = text.lower().count('e')
    i_count = text.lower().count('i')
    o_count = text.lower().count('o')
    u_count = text.lower().count('u')
    prop = (a_count + e_count + i_count + o_count + u_count) / len(text)
    return prop
```

define_function.py

Reminder: if you're using Python 2 rather than Python 3, include this line at the top of your program:

```python
from __future__ import division
```

The first line of the function definition contains a several different elements. We start with the word def, which is short for *define* (writing a function is called *defining* it). Following that we write the name of the function, followed by the names of the argument variables in parentheses. Just like we saw before with normal variables, the function name and the argument names are all **arbitrary** – we can use whatever we like.

The first line ends with a colon, just like the first line of the loops that we were looking at in the previous chapter. And just like loops, this line is followed by a *block* of indented lines – the *function body*. The function

---

1   In fact, we can be a little bit more specific: we can say that the return value will be of type float – a floating point number (i.e. one with a decimal point).

body can have as many lines of code as we like, as long as they all have the same indentation. Within the function body, we can refer to the arguments by using the variable names from the first line. In this case, the variable `text` refers to the string that was passed in as the argument to the function.

The last line of the function causes it to return the proportion that was calculated in the function body. To `return` from a function, we simply write `return` followed by the value that the function should output.

There are a couple of important things to be aware of when writing functions. Firstly, we need to make a clear distinction between *defining* a function, and *running* it (we refer to running a function as *calling* it). The code we've written above will not cause anything to happen when we run it, because we've not actually asked Python to execute the `get_vowel_prop()` function – we have simply defined what it is. The code in the function will not be executed until we call the function like this:

```
get_vowel_prop("It was a rimy morning, and very damp.")
```

If we simply call the function like that, however, then the answer will vanish once it's been calculated. In order to use the function to do something useful, we must either store the result in a variable:

```
vowels = get_vowel_prop("It was a rimy morning, and very damp.")
```

Or use it directly:

```
print("vowel proportion is " + str(get_vowel_prop("It was a ... damp.")))
```

Secondly, it's important to understand that the argument variable `text` does not hold any particular value when the function is defined[1]. Instead, its job is to hold whatever value is given as the argument when the function is called. In this way it's analogous to the loop variables we saw in the previous chapter: loop variables hold a different value each time round the loop, and function argument variables hold a different value each time the function is called.

Finally, be aware that any variables that we create as part of the function only exist inside the function, and cannot be accessed outside. If we try to use a variable that's created inside❶ the function from outside❷:

```
def get_vowel_prop(text):
    a_count = text.lower().count('a')❶
    e_count = text.lower().count('e')
    i_count = text.lower().count('i')
    o_count = text.lower().count('o')
    u_count = text.lower().count('u')
    prop = (a_count + e_count + i_count + o_count + u_count) / len(text)
    return prop

print(a_count)❷
```

We'll get an error:

```
NameError: name 'a_count' is not defined
```

Calling and improving our function

Let's write a small program that uses our new function, to see how it works. We'll call it twice with different inputs. Firstly, we'll try storing the result in a variable before printing it❶, then we'll try printing it directly❷:

---

1   Indeed, it doesn't actually **exist** when the function is defined, only when the function runs.

```
def get_vowel_prop(text):
    ...
    return prop

vowel_prop = get_vowel_prop("abcde")❶
print(vowel_prop)
print(get_vowel_prop("Great Expectations"))❷
```

`calling_function.py`

Looking at the output:

```
0.4
0.388888888889
```

we can see that the first function call works fine – the proportion of vowels is calculated to be 0.4, is stored in the variable `vowel_prop`, then printed. However, the output for the second function call gives an answer with a lot of decimal places – probably more than we need.

We can fix this problem of having too many decimal places by making a couple of changes to the `get_vowel_prop()` function. Python has a built in `round()` function that takes two arguments – the number we want to round, and the number of significant figures. We'll call the `round()` function on the result before we return it❶. Here's the new version of the function, with the same two function calls:

```
def get_vowel_prop(text):
    a_count = text.lower().count('a')
    e_count = text.lower().count('e')
    i_count = text.lower().count('i')
    o_count = text.lower().count('o')
    u_count = text.lower().count('u')
    prop = (a_count + e_count + i_count + o_count + u_count) / len(text)
    return round(prop, 2)❶

vowel_prop = get_vowel_prop("abcde")
print(vowel_prop)
print(get_vowel_prop("Great Expectations"))
```

vowel_prop_improved.py

and now each time the function gives an answer with a sensible number of decimal places:

```
0.4
0.39
```

Encapsulation with functions

Let's pause for a moment and consider what happened in the previous section. We wrote a function, and then wrote some code that used that function. In the process of writing the code that used the function, we discovered a problems with our original function definition – that it returned too many decimal places. **We were then able to go back and change the function definition, without having to make any changes to the code that used the function**.

I've written that last sentence in bold, because it's incredibly important. It's no exaggeration to say that understanding the implications of that sentence is the key to being able to write larger, useful programs. The reason it's so important is that it describes a programming phenomenon that we call *encapsulation*. Encapsulation just means dividing up a complex program into little bits which we can work on independently. In the example above, the code is divided into two parts – the part where we define the function, and the part where we use it – and we can make changes to one part without worrying about the effects on the other part.

This is a very powerful idea, because without it, the size of programs we can write is limited to the number of lines of code we can hold in our head at one time. Some of the example code in the solutions to exercises in the previous chapter were starting to push at this limit already, even for relatively simple problems. By contrast, using functions allows us to build up a complex program from small building blocks, each of which individually is small enough to understand in its entirety.

Because using functions is so important, future solutions to exercises will use them when appropriate, even when it's not explicitly mentioned in the problem text. I encourage you to get into the habit of using functions in your solutions too.

Functions don't always have to take an argument

There's nothing in the rules of Python to say that your function **must** take an argument. It's perfectly possible to define a function with no arguments:

```
def get_a_number():
    return 42
```

but such functions tend not to be very useful. For example, we can write a version of get_vowel_prop() that doesn't require any arguments by setting the value of the text variable inside the function:

```
def get_vowel_prop():
    text = "The Old Curiosity Shop"
    a_count = text.lower().count('a')
    e_count = text.lower().count('e')
    i_count = text.lower().count('i')
    o_count = text.lower().count('o')
    u_count = text.lower().count('u')
    prop = (a_count + e_count + i_count + o_count + u_count) / len(text)
    return round(prop, 2)
```

but that's obviously not very useful, since it will always operate on the same text. Occasionally you may be tempted to write a no-argument function that works like this:

```
def get_vowel_prop():
    a_count = text.lower().count('a')
    e_count = text.lower().count('e')
    i_count = text.lower().count('i')
    o_count = text.lower().count('o')
    u_count = text.lower().count('u')
    prop = (a_count + e_count + i_count + o_count + u_count) / len(text)
    return round(prop, 2)

text = "Oliver Twist"❶
print(get_vowel_prop())
```

At first this seems like a good idea – it works because the function gets the value of the text variable that is set before the function call❶. However, this breaks the encapsulation that we worked so hard to achieve. The function now **only** works if there is a variable called text in the bit of the code where the function is called, so the two pieces of code are no longer independent.

If you find yourself writing code like this, it's usually a good idea to identify which variables from outside the function are being used inside it, and turn them into arguments.

Functions don't always have to return a value

Consider this variation of our function – instead of **returning** the proportion of vowels, this function **prints** it to the screen:

```
def print_vowel_prop(text, sig_figs):
    a_count = text.lower().count('a')
    e_count = text.lower().count('e')
    i_count = text.lower().count('i')
    o_count = text.lower().count('o')
    u_count = text.lower().count('u')
    prop = (a_count + e_count + i_count + o_count + u_count) / len(text)
    print(round(prop, sig_figs) )
```

When you first start writing functions, it's very tempting to do this kind of thing. You think "*OK, I need to calculate and print proportion of vowels – I'll write a function that does both*". The trouble with this approach is that it results in a function that is less flexible. Right now you want to print the proportion of vowels to the screen, but what if you later discover that you need to write it to a file, or use it as part of some other calculation? You'll have to write more functions to carry out these tasks.

The key to designing flexible functions is to recognize that the job *calculate and print the proportion of vowels* is actually two separate jobs – **calculating** the proportion, and **printing** it. Try to write your functions in such a way that they just do one job. You can then easily write code to carry out more complicated jobs by using your simple functions as building blocks.

Functions with multiple arguments

In the section above, we improved our function by making it return a sensible number of significant figures. We can make the function even better though: why not allow it to be called with the number of significant figures as an argument? In the above code, we've picked two significant figures, but there might be situations where we want to see more. Adding the second argument is easy; we just add it to the argument variable list on the first line of the function definition❶, and then use the new argument variable in the call to round()❷:

```
def get_vowel_prop(text, sig_figs):❶
    a_count = text.lower().count('a')
    e_count = text.lower().count('e')
    i_count = text.lower().count('i')
    o_count = text.lower().count('o')
    u_count = text.lower().count('u')
    prop = (a_count + e_count + i_count + o_count + u_count) / len(text)
    return round(prop, sig_figs❶)
```

two_arguments.py

Now look what happens when we call the function with the exact same text as the first argument, but with different numbers of significant figures as the second argument:

```
print(get_vowel_prop("Great Expectations", 1))
print(get_vowel_prop("Great Expectations", 2))
print(get_vowel_prop("Great Expectations", 3))
```

As we increase the number of significant figures, we get more and more accurate return values from our function:

```
0.4
0.39
0.389
```

Functions can be called with named arguments

What do we need to know about a function in order to be able to use it? We need to know what the return value and type is, and we need to know the number and type of the arguments. For the examples we've seen so far in this book, we also need to know the **order** of the arguments. For instance, to use the open() function we need to know that the name of the file comes first, followed by the mode of the file. And to use our two-argument version of get_vowel_prop() described above, we need to know that the input text comes first, followed by the number of significant figures.

There's a feature in Python called *keyword arguments* which allows us to call functions in a slightly different way. Instead of giving a list of arguments in parentheses:

```
get_vowel_prop("Great Expectations", 2)
```

we can supply a list of argument variable names and values joined by equals signs:

```
get_vowel_prop(text="Great Expectations", sig_figs=2)
```

This style of calling functions[1] has several advantages. It doesn't rely on the order of arguments, so we can use whichever order we prefer. These two statements behave identically:

```
get_vowel_prop(text="Great Expectations", sig_figs=2)
get_vowel_prop(sig_figs=2, text="Great Expectations")
```

It's also clearer to read what's happening when the argument names are given explicitly.

We can even mix and match the two styles of calling – the following are all identical:

---

1   It works with methods too, including all the ones we've seen so far.

```
get_vowel_prop("Great Expectations", 2)
get_vowel_prop(text="Great Expectations", sig_figs=2)
get_vowel_prop("Great Expectations", sig_figs=2)
```

`keyword_arguments.py`

Although we're not allowed to start off with keyword arguments then switch back to normal – this will cause an error:

```
get_at_content(text="Great Expectations", 2)
```

Keyword arguments can be particularly useful for functions and methods that have a lot of arguments, and we'll use them where appropriate in the examples and exercise solutions in the rest of this book.

Function arguments can have defaults

We've encountered function arguments with defaults before, when we were discussing opening files in chapter 3. Recall that the open() function takes two arguments – a file name and a mode string – but that if we call it with **just** a file name it uses a default value for the mode string. We can easily take advantage of this feature in our own functions – we simply specify the default value in the first line of the function definition. Here's a version of our get_vowel_prop() function where the default number of significant figures is two:

```
def get_vowel_prop(text, sig_figs=2):
    a_count = text.lower().count('a')
    e_count = text.lower().count('e')
    i_count = text.lower().count('i')
    o_count = text.lower().count('o')
    u_count = text.lower().count('u')
    prop = (a_count + e_count + i_count + o_count + u_count) / len(text)
    return round(prop, sig_figs)
```

The only change that we've made to the code is to add =2 after the
sig_figs variable in the definition line. Now we have the best of both
worlds. If the function is called with two arguments, it will use the
number of significant figures specified; if it's called with one argument, it
will use the default of two significant figures. Let's see some examples:

```
print(get_vowel_prop("Great Expectations"))
print(get_vowel_prop("Great Expectations", 3))
print(get_vowel_prop("Great Expectations", sig_figs=4))
```

default_argument_values.py

The function takes care of filling in the default value for sig_figs for
the first function call where none is supplied:

```
0.39
0.389
0.3889
```

Function argument defaults allow us to write very flexible functions
which can have varying numbers of arguments. It only makes sense to use
them for arguments where a sensible default can be chosen – there's no
point specifying a default for the text argument in our example. They
are particularly useful for functions where some of the options are only
going to be used infrequently.

Testing functions

When writing code of any type, it's important to periodically check that your code does what you intend it to do. If you look back over the solutions to exercises from the first few chapters, you can see that we generally test our code at each step by printing some output to the screen and checking that it looks OK. For example, in chapter 2 when we were first calculating vowel content, we used a very short test string to verify that our code worked before running it on the real input.

The reason we used a test string was that, because it was so short, we could easily work out the answer by eye and compare it to the answer given by our code. This idea – running code on a test input and comparing the result to an answer **that we know is right** – is such a useful one that Python has a built in tool for expressing it: assert. An assertion consists of the word assert, followed by a call to our function, then **two** equals signs, then the result that we expect[1].

For example, we know that if we run our get_vowel_prop() function on the text string "ab" we should get an answer of 0.5. This assertion will test whether that's the case:

```
assert get_vowel_prop("ab") == 0.5
```

Notice the two equals signs – we'll learn the reason behind that in the next chapter. The way that assertion statements work is very simple; if an assertion turns out to be false (i.e. if Python executes our function on the input "ab" and the answer **isn't** 0.5) then the program will stop and we will get an AssertionError.

---

1   In fact, assertions can include any conditional statement; we'll learn about those in the next chapter.

Assertions are useful in a number of ways. They provide a means for us to check whether our functions are working as intended and therefore help us track down errors in our programs. If we get some unexpected output from a program that uses a particular function, and the assertion tests for that function all pass, then we can be confident that the error doesn't lie in the function but in the code that calls it.

Assertions also let us modify a function and check that we haven't introduced any errors. If we have a function that passes a series of assertion tests, and we make some changes to it, we can rerun the assertion tests and, assuming they all pass, be confident that we haven't broken the function[1].

Assertions are also useful as a form of documentation. By including a collection of assertion tests alongside a function, we can show exactly what output is expected from a given input.

Finally, we can use assertions to test the behaviour of our function for unusual inputs. For example, what will happen if we try to call `get_vowel_prop()` with an empty string as the input?

```
get_vowel_prop("")
```

The answer is that we get an error:

```
    prop = (a_count + e_count + i_count + o_count + u_count) / len(text)
ZeroDivisionError: division by zero
```

because Python tries to divide the number of vowels by the length of the string, which is zero. All programming languages are very unhappy when you ask them to divide something by zero, because the result is undefined. To fix this problem, we have to decide what

---

1   This idea is very similar to a process in software development called *regression testing*.

`get_vowel_prop()` should do if we give it an empty string as the input. One option would be to make it return -1, since a negative number can't be generated by the function for any normal input. We can write an assertion to **test** this behaviour:

```
assert get_vowel_prop("") == -1
```

but editing the function to actually **implement** that behaviour will have to wait for the next chapter where we discuss conditions.

It's common to group a collection of assertions for a particular function together to test for the correct behaviour on different types of input. Here's an example for `get_vowel_prop()` which shows a range of different types of behaviour:

```
assert get_vowel_prop('a') == 1
assert get_vowel_prop('b') == 0
assert get_vowel_prop('abab') == 0.5
assert get_vowel_prop('abb') == 0.33
assert get_vowel_prop('abb', 5) == 0.33333
```

test_function.py

Recap

In this chapter, we've seen how packaging up code into functions helps us to manage the complexity of large programs and promote code reuse. We learned how to define and call our own functions along with various new ways to supply arguments to functions. We also looked at a couple of things that are possible in Python, but rarely advisable – writing functions without arguments or return values. Finally, we explored the use of assertions to test our functions, and discussed how we can use them to catch errors before they become a problem.

The remaining chapters in this book will make use of functions in both the examples and the exercise solutions, so make sure you are comfortable with the new ideas from this chapter before moving on.

Exercises

Proportion of letters

Modify the `get_vowel_prop()` function so that it can work on **any** collection of letters, not just vowels. You'll need to add another argument to the function, which will be the list of letters to include in the count. Your function should round all results to two significant figures. Use this set of assert statements to test your function:

```
assert get_letter_prop('Great Expectations', ['e']) == 0.17
assert get_letter_prop('Great Expectations', ['e', 't']) == 0.33
assert get_letter_prop("Great Expectations", ['G', 'N']) == 0.11
```

Add a default for the second argument (the list of letters), so that if you call the function with only the text string it returns the proportion of vowels:

```
assert get_letter_prop("Great Expectations") == 0.39
```

Reminder: if you're using Python 2 rather than Python 3, include this line at the top of your program:

```
from __future__ import division
```

Solutions

Proportion of letters

This exercise reflects a very common situation in programming. We have written a function that does a useful job – calculates the proportion of vowels in a piece of text. After using the function for a while, we realize that the problem it solves is just a specific example of a much more general problem – calculating the proportion of an arbitrary set of letters in a piece of text – so we modify the function to be more flexible.

Let's start with the version of get_vowel_prop() that always returns two significant figures, since that's part of the exercise description:

```
def get_vowel_prop(text):
    a_count = text.lower().count('a')
    e_count = text.lower().count('e')
    i_count = text.lower().count('i')
    o_count = text.lower().count('o')
    u_count = text.lower().count('u')
    prop = (a_count + e_count + i_count + o_count + u_count) / len(text)
    return round(prop, 2)
```

We know from the exercise description that the eventual solution will be a function that takes a list of letters as one of its arguments, so a good start would be to replace the repetitive letter counting code with a list and a loop. We'll create a list❶ to store the vowels and a loop❷ to iterate over them. For now, let's just print the count for each vowel so that we can check whether the code is working:

```
def get_vowel_prop(text):
    letters = ['a', 'e', 'i', 'o', 'u']❶
    for letter in letters:❷
        letter_count = text.count(letter)
        print(letter_count)

get_vowel_prop('Great Expectations')
```

If you take a close look at the code above, you'll see something interesting – the lines of code inside the function definition are indented (just as we've seen before), but the lines of code inside the for loop are indented **twice** – once for the function, and once for the for loop. This is the first time we've seen multiple levels of indentation, but it's very common once we start working with larger programs – whenever we have one block of code nested inside another, we'll have this type of indentation.

Python is quite happy to have as many levels of indentation as needed, but you'll need to keep careful track of which lines of code belong at which level. If you find yourself writing a piece of code that requires more than three levels of indentation, it's generally an indication that that piece of code should be turned into a function.

When we run the code above, we can see that it gives us counts for the each vowel in the order that we specified:

```
2
2
1
1
0
```

Immediately we can see a problem: there are three **e**'s in "*Great Expectations*", but the function is only reporting two. It's the old problem of case sensitivity; the letters are in lower case so they're not counting the upper case **E** at the start of "*Expectations*". To fix this, we can use `lower()` to turn the text into lower case before we do the count❶:

```
def get_vowel_prop(text):
    letters = ['a', 'e', 'i', 'o', 'u']
    for letter in letters:
        letter_count = text.lower().count(letter)❶
        print(letter_count)

get_vowel_prop('Great Expectations')
```

and now the output is correct:

```
2
3
1
1
0
```

The next step is to add up all the individual letter counts. It's not immediately obvious how to do this. In the old version of the code, each count was stored in a separate variable, so we could just add them all together:

```
a_count + e_count + i_count ...
```

but in this new version which uses a loop, we only have access to the count for a single letter each time round the loop. The solution is to create a new variable❶ to hold a running total, and update it each time round the loop❷:

```
def get_vowel_prop(text):
    letters = ['a', 'e', 'i', 'o', 'u']
    total = 0❶
    for letter in letters:
        letter_count = text.lower().count(letter)
        total = total + letter_count❷
        print(total)

get_vowel_prop('Great Expectations')
```

The line that updates the total looks strange when we read it for the first time, since the total variable appears on both sides of the equals sign:

```
total = total + letter_count
```

but this is a common thing to do in programming. It works because Python evaluates the right hand side of the equals sign first (i.e. takes the current value of `total` and adds `letter_count`) before storing the result back into total. If we look at the output from this code we can see how the value of `total` increases as we add the count for each vowel in turn:

```
2
5
6
7
7
```

To turn this back into a useful function, we have to make a few changes. Firstly, we're not interested in the count for each individual letter, just the total, so we can just deal with the final value of the `total` variable after the loop has finished. Secondly, we want the proportion of vowels, not the count. Thirdly, we want to return the proportion, not print it.

We can fix all three of these issues with two lines. First we take the total and divide by the length to get the proportion❶, then we round the proportion to 2 significant figures and return it❷:

```
def get_vowel_prop(text):
    letters = ['a', 'e', 'i', 'o', 'u']
    total = 0
    for letter in letters:
        letter_count = text.lower().count(letter)
        total = total + letter_count
    proportion = total / len(text)❶
    return round(proportion, 2)❷

print(get_vowel_prop('Great Expectations'))
```

This seems like a lot of work only to end up with a function that behaves just the same as the version we started with! However, by creating a list containing the letters we want to count, we have made it very easy to turn the list of letters into an argument. We only need to make a single change: remove the definition of the letters variable from the function, and add the letters variable as an argument in the function definition:

```
def get_letters_prop(text, letters):
    total = 0
    for letter in letters:
        letter_count = text.lower().count(letter)
        total = total + letter_count
    proportion = total / len(text)
    return round(proportion, 2)
```

This single change[1] allows us to call the function with any list of letters:

```
print(get_letters_prop('Great Expectations', ['x', 't']))
print(get_letters_prop('Great Expectations', ['e', 'p', 'r']))
```

---

1   Notice that we've also changed the name of the function to reflect the fact that it doesn't just work on vowels any more, but that's just a cosmetic change.

and get back an answer:

```
0.22
0.28
```

This seems like a pretty good solution to the exercise, so let's try it out by running the assert statements from the exercise description:

```
assert get_letter_prop('Great Expectations', ['e']) == 0.17
assert get_letter_prop('Great Expectations', ['e', 't']) == 0.33
assert get_letter_prop("Great Expectations", ['G', 'N']) == 0.11
```

The output from running these statements shows that our function is failing on the third assertion:

```
    assert get_letter_prop("Great Expectations", ['G', 'N']) == 0.11
AssertionError
```

and if we take a close look at the inputs we can see why. In the third assertion, the list of letters is in upper case, and in our function, we are searching for them in a lower case version of the input text. Fixing the bug is straightforward: we can just call lower() on the letter as well as on the input text❶:

```
def get_letters_prop(text, letters):
    total = 0
    for letter in letters:
        letter_count = text.lower().count(letter.lower())❶
        total = total + letter_count
    proportion = total / len(text)
    return round(proportion, 2)
```

and now all three tests pass without error.

The final step is to implement the default behaviour: if the function is called without a list of letters, it should return the proportion of vowels. This sounds like a tricky requirement, but if we take advantage of Python's ability to have default function arguments, it's easy – we just add the default in the function definition line❶:

```
def get_letters_prop(text, letters=['a', 'e', 'i', 'o', 'u']):❶
    ...
```

Here's the final code, which contains the function along with the collection of `assert` statements:

```
from __future__ import division

def get_letter_prop(text, letters=['a', 'e', 'i', 'o', 'u']):
    total = 0
    for letter in letters:
        # convert to lower case and count the letter
        letter_count = text.lower().count(letter.lower())
        # update the total count
        total = total + letter_count

    # calculate the proportion, round it, and return it
    proportion = total / len(text)
    return round(proportion, 2)


assert get_letter_prop('Great Expectations', ['e']) == 0.17
assert get_letter_prop('Great Expectations', ['e', 't']) == 0.33
assert get_letter_prop("Great Expectations", ['G', 'N']) == 0.11
assert get_letter_prop("Great Expectations") == 0.39
```

letter_proportions.py

We began this exercise by thinking about how the problem of counting **vowels** in a piece of text was just an example of the more general problem of counting a **set of letters** in a piece of text. It's interesting to note that we can apply the same logic again: given that letters are just strings that happen to be one character long, the problem of counting a **set of letters** in a bit of text is just an example of the more general problem of counting a **set of strings** in a bit of text. So if we modify our function a bit to take into account the length of each string we're looking for❶:

```
def get_string_prop(text, strings=['a', 'e', 'i', 'o', 'u']):
    total = 0
    for string in strings:
        string_count = text.lower().count(string.lower())
        total = total + string_count * len(string)❶
    proportion = total / len(text)
    return round(proportion, 2)
```

it's actually capable of counting the proportion of a piece of text that's made up of any set of strings. For instance, we can take the entire text of *Great Expectations*[1]:

```
ge = open("great_expectations_complete.txt").read()
```

and ask what proportion of it is made up of some short common words:

```
print(get_string_prop(ge, [' and ', ' to ', ' the ', ' of ', ' a ']))
```

```
0.12
```

This insight is an example of something that happens quite often in programming; writing a program to solve a particular problem helps us to understand it and see it in a new way.

---

1   We'll be playing with this file in chapter 7, so you can find it in the chapter_7 exercises folder if you want to try this out.

What have we learned?

Although this exercise is about analysing text, the principles of separating code in functions applies to all types of programming problems. The process of modifying a function that we used to solve the exercise is one that's very commonly used in real life programming, and we were able to use advanced features like default argument values.

▌6:   Conditional tests

Programs need to make decisions

If we look back at the examples and exercises in previous chapters, something that stands out is the lack of decision making. We've gone from doing simple calculations on individual bits of data to carrying out more complicated procedures on collections of data, but each bit of data (a name, a sentence, a letter, or a number) has been treated identically.

Real life problems, however, often require our programs to act as decision makers: to examine a piece of data and decide what to do with it. In this chapter, we'll see how to do that using *conditional statements*. Conditional statements are features of Python that allow us to build decision points in our code. They allow our programs to decide which out of a number of possible courses of action to take – instructions like *allow the player through the door if the have the correct key* or *display this page if the status is 'published'*.

Before we can start using conditional statements, however, we need to understand *conditions*.

Conditions, True and False

A *condition* is simply a bit of code that can produce a true or false answer. The easiest way to understand how conditions work in Python is try out a few examples. The following code prints out the result of testing (or *evaluating*) a bunch of different conditions – some mathematical examples, some using string methods, and one for testing if a value is included in a list:

```
print(3 == 5) # False
print(3 > 5) # False
print(3 <=5) # True
print(len("Great Expectations") > 5) # True
print("Great Expectations".count("e") > 1) # True
print("Bleak House".startswith("B")) # True
print("Little Dorrit".endswith("abc")) # False
print("NOVEL".isupper()) # True
print("NOVEL".islower()) # False
print("the" in ["and", "a", "the", "it"]) # True
```

`print_conditions.py`

Take a look at the output from this program:

```
False
False
True
...
```

What's actually being printed here? At first glance, it looks like we're printing the strings "True" and "False", but those strings don't appear anywhere in our code. What is actually being printed is the special built in values that Python uses to represent true and false – they are capitalized so that we know they're these special values.

We can show that these values are special by trying to print them. The following code runs without errors (note the absence of quotation marks):

```
print(True)
print(False)
```

whereas trying to print arbitrary unquoted words:

```
print(Hello)
```

causes a `NameError`.

There's a wide range of things that we can include in conditions, and it would be impossible to give an exhaustive list here. The basic building blocks are:

- equals (represented by ==)

- greater and less than (represented by > and <)

- greater and less than or equal to (represented by >= and <=)

- not equal (represented by !=)

- is a value in a list (represented by in)

Many data types also provide methods that return `True` or `False` values, which are often a lot more convenient to use than the building blocks above. We've already seen a few in the code sample above: for example, strings have a `startswith()` method that returns `True` if the string starts with the string given as an argument. We'll mention these true/false methods when they come up. Notice that the test for equality is **two** equals signs, not one. Forgetting the second equals sign will cause an error.

Now that we know how to express tests as conditions, let's see what we can do with them.

if statements

The simplest kind of conditional statement is an `if` statement. Hopefully the syntax is fairly easy to understand:

```
birth_year = 1812
if birth_year < 1900:
    print("The author was born before the 20th century")
```

We write the word if, followed by a condition, and end the first line with a colon. There follows a block of indented lines of code (the *body* of the if statement), which will only be executed if the condition is true. This colon-plus-block pattern should be familiar to you from the chapters on loops and functions.

Most of the time, we want to use an if statement to test a property of some variable whose value we don't know at the time when we are writing the program. The example above is obviously useless, as the value of the birth_year variable is not going to change!

Here's a slightly more interesting example: we'll define a list of character names and print out just the ones that start with the letter **M**:

```
names = ["Pip", "Joe", "Magwitch", "Matthew", "Estella"]
for name in names:
    if name.startswith('M'):
        print(name)
```

print_names.py

Notice how the print() line is indented twice – once because it's inside the for loop, and once because it's inside the if statement.

Looking at the output allows us to check that this works as intended:

```
Magwitch
Matthew
```

else statements

Closely related to the `if` statement is the `else` statement. The examples above use a **yes/no** type of decision making: should we print the character name or not? Often we need an **either/or** type of decision, where we have two possible actions to take. To do this, we can add on an `else` clause after the end of the body of an `if` statement:

```
birth_year = 1812
if birth_year < 1900:
    print("The author was born before the 20th century")
else:
    print("The author was born after the start of the 20th century")
```

The `else` statement doesn't have any condition of its own – rather, the `else` statement body is executed when the `if` statement to which it's attached is **not** executed.

Here's an example which uses `if` and `else` to split up a list of character names into two different files – names that start with **M** go into the first file, and all other names go into the second file:

```
file1 = open("one.txt", "w")
file2 = open("two.txt", "w")
names = ["Pip", "Joe", "Magwitch", "Matthew", "Estella"]
for name in names:
    if name.startswith('M'):
        file1.write(name + "\n")
    else:
        file2.write(name + "\n")
```

`write_names.py`

Notice how there are multiple indentation levels as before, but that the `if` and `else` statements are at the **same** level.

elif statements

What if we have more than two possible branches? For example, say we want three files of character names: ones that start with **M**, ones that start with **E**, and all others. We could have a second if statement❶ nested inside the else clause of the first if statement:

```
file1 = open("one.txt", "w")
file2 = open("two.txt", "w")
file3 = open("three.txt", "w")

names = ["Pip", "Joe", "Magwitch", "Matthew", "Estella"]
for name in names:
    if name.startswith('M'):
        file1.write(name + "\n")
    else:
        if name.startswith('E'):❶
            file2.write(name + "\n")
        else:
            file3.write(name + "\n")
```

This works, but is difficult to read – we can quickly see that we need an extra level of indentation for every additional choice we want to include. To get round this, Python has an elif statement, which merges together else and if and allows us to rewrite the above example in a much more elegant way:

```
file1 = open("one.txt", "w")
file2 = open("two.txt", "w")
file3 = open("three.txt", "w")

names = ["Pip", "Joe", "Magwitch", "Matthew", "Estella"]
for name in names:
    if name.startswith('M'):
        file1.write(name + "\n")
    elif name.startswith('E'):
        file2.write(name + "\n")
    else:
        file3.write(name + "\n")
```

write_names_elif.py

Notice how this version of the code only needs two levels of indention. In fact, using `elif` we can have any number of branches and still only require a single level of indentation:

```
for name in names:
    if name.startswith('A'):
        # do something
    elif name.startswith('B'):
        # do something
    elif name.startswith('C'):
        # do something
    elif name.startswith('D'):
        # do something
    elif name.startswith('E'):
        # do something
    else:
        # do something
```

Note the order of the statements in the example above; we always start with an `if` and end with an `else`, and all the `elif` statements go in the middle. This kind of `if`/`elif`/`else` structure is very useful when we have several mutually exclusive options. In the example above, only one branch can be true for each name – a string can't start with both **A** and **B**. If we have a situation where the branches are not mutually exclusive – i.e.

where more than one branch can be taken – then we simply need a series of `if` statements:

```
for name in names:
    if name.startswith('E'):
        # do something
    if name.endswith('a'):
        # do something
    if len(name) == 7:
        # do something
    if name.count('l') > 2:
        # do something
```

Notice how in the above example, the four conditions are **not** mutually exclusive – it's possible for several of the conditions to be true for a given name (for example, *"Estella"* satisfies the first three conditions – it starts with **E**, ends with **a**, and is seven characters long).

while loops

Here's one final thing we can do with conditions: use them to determine when to stop a loop. In chapter 4 we learned about loops that *iterate over* a collection of items (like a list, a string or a file). Python has another type of loop called a `while` loop. Rather than running a set number of times, a `while` loop runs until some condition is met. For example, here's a bit of code that increments a `count` variable by one each time round the loop, stopping when the `count` variable reaches ten:

```
count = 0
while count<10:
    print(count)
    count = count + 1
```

Because normal loops in Python are so powerful[1], while loops are used much less frequently in Python than in other languages, so we won't discuss them further.

Building up complex conditions

What if we wanted to express a condition that was made up of several parts? Imagine we want to go through our list of names and print out only the ones that start with **M** and end with **h**. We could use two nested if statements:

```
names = ["Pip", "Joe", "Magwitch", "Matthew", "Estella"]
for name in names:
    if name.startswith('M'):
        if name.endswith('h'):
            print(name)
```

but this brings in an extra, unneeded level of indention. A better way is to join up the two conditions with and to make a complex condition:

```
names = ["Pip", "Joe", "Magwitch", "Matthew", "Estella"]
for name in names:
    if name.startswith('M') and name.endswith('h'):
        print(name)
```

names_and.py

This version is better in two ways: it doesn't require the extra level of indentation, and the condition reads in a very natural way. We can also use or to join up two conditions, to produce a complex condition that will be true if either of the two simple conditions are true:

---

1   E.g. the example code here could be better accomplished with a range().

```
names = ["Pip", "Joe", "Magwitch", "Matthew", "Estella"]
for name in names:
    if name.startswith('M') or name.startswith('J'):
        print(name)
```

names_or.py

We can even join up complex conditions to make more complex conditions – here's an example which prints names if they start with either **M** or **J** and are at least 4 letters long:

```
names = ["Pip", "Joe", "Magwitch", "Matthew", "Estella"]
for name in names:
    if (name.startswith('M') or name.startswith('J')) and len(name)>=4:
        print(name)
```

names_complex.py

Notice how we have to include parentheses in the above example to avoid ambiguity. If we have three simple conditions represented by X, Y and Z, then the complex condition

```
(X or Y) and Z
```

is not the same as the complex condition

```
X or (Y and Z)
```

Finally, we can negate any type of condition by prefixing it with the word not. This example will print out names that start with **M** and **don't** end with **h**:

```
names = ["Pip", "Joe", "Magwitch", "Matthew", "Estella"]
for name in names:
    if name.startswith('M') and not name.endswith('h'):
        print(name)
```

names_not.py

By using a combination of and, or and not (along with parentheses where necessary) we can build up arbitrarily complex conditions. These three words are collectively known as *boolean operators* and crop up in a lot of places. For example, if you wanted to search the internet for information on using Python to store recipes, but didn't want to see pages that talked about cooking snakes, you might do a Google search for *"Python recipes -snake"*. This is actually a complex condition just like the ones above – Google automatically adds **and** between words, and uses the hyphen to mean **not**. So you're asking for pages that mention Python **and** recipes but **not** snakes.

Writing true/false functions

Sometimes we want to write a function that can be used in a condition. This is very easy to do – we just make sure that our function always returns either True or False. Remember that True and False are built in values in Python, so they can be passed around, stored in variables, and returned, just like numbers or strings.

Here's a function that determines whether or not a word has a lot of vowels (we'll say that a word has a lot of vowels if more than half its letters are vowels). It's based on the vowel counting examples from previous chapters, but instead of returning the proportion of vowels it uses the proportion to decide whether to return True or False:

```
def is_vowel_rich(word):
    letters = ['a', 'e', 'i', 'o', 'u']
    total = 0
    for letter in letters:
        letter_count = word.lower().count(letter)
        total = total + letter_count
    proportion = total / len(word)
    if proportion >= 0.5:
        return True
    else:
        return False
```

boolean_function.py

We'll test this function on a few words to see if it works:

```
print(is_vowel_rich("ignuana"))
print(is_vowel_rich("lizard"))
```

The output shows that the function returns `True` or `False` just like the other conditions we've been looking at:

```
True
False
```

Therefore we can use our function in an `if` statement – for instance, we could take the opening sentence of *A Tale of Two Cities* and print just the vowel-rich words:

```
def is_vowel_rich(word):
    ...

text = "It was the best of times ... comparison only."

for word in text.split(" "):
    if is_vowel_rich(word):
        print(word)
```

use_boolean_function.py

```
period
so
like
some
of
noisiest
```

Because the last four lines of our function are devoted to evaluating a condition and returning `True` or `False`, we can write a slightly more compact version. In this example we evaluate the condition, and then return the result right away❶:

```
def is_vowel_rich(word):
    letters = ['a', 'e', 'i', 'o', 'u']
    total = 0
    for letter in letters:
        letter_count = word.lower().count(letter)
        total = total + letter_count
    proportion = total / len(word)
    return proportion >= 0.5❶
```

This is a little more concise, and also easier to read once you're familiar with the idiom.

Recap

In this chapter, we've dealt with two things: conditions, and the statements that use them.

We've seen how simple conditions can be joined together to make more complex ones, and how the concepts of truth and falsehood are built in to Python on a fundamental level. We've also seen how we can incorporate `True` and `False` in our own functions in a way that allows them to be used as part of conditions.

We've been introduced to four different tools that use conditions – `if`, `else`, `elif`, and `while` – in approximate order of usefulness. You'll probably find, in the programs that you write and in your solutions to the exercises in this book, that you use `if` and `else` very frequently, `elif` occasionally, and `while` almost never.

Exercises

In the *chapter_6* folder in the exercises download, you'll find a text file called *data.csv*, containing information on a number of works by Charles Dickens. Each line of the file contains the following fields for a single work in this order: title, publication date, type, length.

The fields are separated by commas (hence the name of the file – *csv* stands for Comma Separated Values, which we encountered in chapter 4). Think of it as a representation of a table in a spreadsheet – each line is a row, and each field in a line is a column. All the exercises for this chapter use the data from this file.

Reminder: if you're using Python 2 rather than Python 3, include this line at the top of your programs:

```
from __future__ import division
```

Novels and novellas

Print out the titles of all works whose type is either *novel* or *novella*.

Date range

Print out the titles of all works published between 1839 and 1845.

Length and title

Print out the titles of all works shorter than 300,000 words whose title is made up of at least 30% vowels.

Complex condition

Print out the titles for all works whose title begins with either "The" or "A", **except** the ones that are collections of short stories.

Short medium long

For each work, print out a message giving the title and saying whether it is short (less than 100,000 words), medium (between 100,000 and 300,000 words) or long (more than 300,000 words).

Solutions

Novels and novellas

These exercises are somewhat more complicated than previous ones, and they're going to require material from multiple different chapters to solve. The first problem is to deal with the format of the data file. Open it up in a text editor and take a look before continuing.

We know that we're going to have to open the file (chapter 3) and process the contents line by line (chapter 4). To deal with each line, we'll have to split it to make a list of columns (chapter 4), then apply the condition (this chapter) in order to figure out whether or not we should print it. Here's a program that will read each line from the file, split it using commas as the delimiter, then assign each of the four columns to a variable and print the title:

```
data = open("data.csv")

for line in data:

    # split the line up
    columns = line.rstrip("\n").split(",")

    # assign the columns to variables
    title = columns[0]
    year = columns[1]
    type = columns[2]
    length = columns[3]

    print(title)
```

Notice that we use `rstrip()` to remove the newline from the end of the current line before splitting it. We know the order of the fields in the line because they were mentioned in the exercise description, so we can easily assign them to the four variables. This program doesn't do anything useful, but we can check the output to confirm that it gets the titles right:

```
The Pickwick Papers
The Mudfog Papers
Oliver Twist
A Christmas Carol
Bleak House
```

Now we can add in the condition. We want to print the title if the type is **either** *novel* **or** *novella*. If the type is something else, then we don't want to do anything. This is a **yes/no** type decision, so we need an if statement:

```
data = open("data.csv")

for line in data:

    # split the line up
    columns = line.rstrip("\n").split(",")

    # assign the columns to variables
    title = columns[0]
    year = columns[1]
    type = columns[2]
    length = columns[3]

    if type == 'novel' or type == 'novella':
        print(title)
```

novels.py

We can check the output we get:

```
The Pickwick Papers
Oliver Twist
A Christmas Carol
Bleak House
```

against the contents of the file, and confirm that the program is working. This last step is important, by the way – it's not enough simply to check that the program runs without producing any errors: we have to check that the titles are correct.

Date range

We can reuse a large part of the code from the previous exercise to help solve this one. We have another complex condition: we only want to print titles for works published between 1839 and 1845 – in other words, works whose year is greater than or equal to 1839 **and** less than or equal to 1845.

Once we've figured out the condition, that's the only bit of the program we need to change❶ – the rest of the program (opening and reading the file, splitting the lines, assigning variables, etc.) can remain the same:

```
data = open("data.csv")

for line in data:

    # split the line up
    columns = line.rstrip("\n").split(",")

    # assign the columns to variables
    title = columns[0]
    year = columns[1]
    type = columns[2]
    length = columns[3]

    if year >= 1839 and year <= 1845:❶
        print(title)
```

This code looks OK, and runs without errors, but it doesn't print any titles. A quick look at the data file tells us that there are two works –

Oliver Twist and *A Christmas Carol* – that fit the dates, so there should be two titles printed.

The problem we have run into is the same one we encountered in the extracting speech exercise of chapter 4 – the result of calling the split() method on a string is a list of strings, so the year variable actually stores a string rather than a number. As before, the fix is easy: we use the int() function to turn the string into a number. The best place to do it is at the point where we create the year variable❶ , and we will do the same for the length variable❷, since we know that it should be a number as well:

```
data = open("data.csv")

for line in data:

    # split the line up
    columns = line.rstrip("\n").split(",")

    # assign the columns to variables
    title = columns[0]
    year = int(columns[1])❶
    type = columns[2]
    length = int(columns[3])❷

    if year >= 1839 and year <= 1845:
        print(title)
```

date_range.py

Now the program runs and gives us the output we want:

```
Oliver Twist
A Christmas Carol
```

For this type of condition, where we've got an upper and lower bound, there's a little trick to make it more readable. We can write the condition like this:

```
1839 <= year <= 1845
```

which Python treats exactly the same way, but is easier for us humans to read.

Length and title

This exercise has a complex condition like the previous ones, but it also requires us to do a bit more calculation – we need to be able to calculate the proportion of vowels for each title. Rather than starting from scratch, we'll simply use the function that we wrote in the previous chapter and include it at the start of the program. Once we've done that, it's just a case of using the output from `get_vowel_prop()` as part of the condition:

```
def get_vowel_prop(text):
    ...


data = open("data.csv")

for line in data:

    # split the line up
    columns = line.rstrip("\n").split(",")

    # assign the columns to variables
    title = columns[0]
    year = int(columns[1])
    type = columns[2]
    length = int(columns[3])


    if get_vowel_prop(title) >= 0.3 and length < 300000:
        print(title)
```

length_title.py

Complex condition

There are no calculations to carry out for this exercise – the complexity comes from the fact that there are three components to the condition, and they have to be joined together in the right way:

```
data = open("data.csv")

for line in data:

    # split the line up
    columns = line.rstrip("\n").split(",")

    # assign the columns to variables
    title = columns[0]
    year = int(columns[1])
    type = columns[2]
    length = int(columns[3])


    if (title.startswith("The") or title.startswith("A")) and type !=
'short stories':
        print(title)
```

complex_condition.py

The line containing the if statement is quite long, so it wraps around
onto the next line on this page, but it's still just a single line in the
program file. There are two different ways to express the requirement
that the type is not "*short stories*". In the above example we've used the
not-equals sign (!=) but we could also have used the not boolean
operator:

```
if (title.startswith("The") or title.startswith("A")) and not type ==
'short stories':
```

Short medium long

Now we come to an exercise that requires the use of multiple branches.
We have three different options for each work – short, medium, and long
– and they are mutually exclusive: a given work cannot be both short and

long. Therefore, we need an `if..elif..else` section to handle the conditions:

```
data = open("data.csv")

for line in data:

    # split the line up
    columns = line.rstrip("\n").split(",")

    # assign the columns to variables
    title = columns[0]
    year = int(columns[1])
    type = columns[2]
    length = int(columns[3])


    if length < 100000:
        print(title + " is short")
    elif 100000 <= length <= 300000:❶
        print(title + " is medium")
    else:
        print(title + " is long")
```

short_medium_long.py

Although the logic is hopefully easy to follow, there are a couple of interesting things going on here. Notice how we use the upper/lower bound trick to test if the length is between 100,000 words and 300,000 words❶. Also, note that we don't need a condition to test for long works – if a given work doesn't fall into the short or medium categories, then it must be long by definition.

When dealing with interval data like this, often it's tempting to just use a bunch of if statements:

```
    if length < 100000:
        print(title + " is short")
    if 100000 <= length <= 300000:
        print(title + " is medium")
    if length > 300000:
        print(title + " is long")
```

This approach will work, but is less efficient, because the computer has to check all three `if` statements each time round the loop. In contrast, when we use `if..elif..else` Python knows that it can skip the second condition if the first one is true.

Checking the output confirms that the conditions are working:

```
The Pickwick Papers is long
The Mudfog Papers is long
Oliver Twist is medium
A Christmas Carol is short
Bleak House is long
```

What have we learned?

As with many of the exercises in this book, the output from these probably isn't very exciting unless you're really interested in 19th century literature. However, take a moment to think about the general type of problem we have been solving – taking a collection of structured data and filtering it based on various criteria. Many real life problems fall into this category – imagine, for example, taking a list of apartments for rent and finding just the ones within your budget in the area you want to live, or taking a list of your digital photos and finding just the ones taken on your birthday.

It's also interesting to note that the solutions to these exercises will work for input files of any size with absolutely no changes in the code. To keep the examples simple, we have been working with a data file with just five rows, but we could take a similar file containing details of millions of books and, as long as the order of the fields remained the same, our solutions would work just as well.

Finally, it's worth noting that most spreadsheet programs (e.g. Google Sheets, Microsoft Excel, GNU calc, etc.) are capable of saving files in CSV format. If you have some information stored in a spreadsheet, try saving it as CSV, then come up with a couple of simple questions and try writing programs to answer them.

7: Dictionaries

Counting words

Suppose we want to count the number of times the word 'and' appears in the text of *Great Expectations*. Carrying out the calculation is quite straightforward, assuming we have a file that contains the text of the book:

```
ge = open("great_expectations_complete.txt").read()
and_count = ge.count(' and ')
```

We just open and read the file, then use the `count()` method to get our answer. Notice that the string we search for starts and ends with a space in order to avoid counting words like "**hand**kerchief".

How will our code change if we want to also count the number of occurrences of some other common words? We'll add a new variable for each word we want to count:

```
ge = open("great_expectations_complete.txt").read()
and_count = ge.count(' and ')
the_count = ge.count(' the ')
to_count  = ge.count(' to ')
of_count  = ge.count(' of ')
```

and now our code is starting to look rather repetitive. It's not too bad if we only have four words, but imagine that we want to make a count for every single word in the dictionary from **a** to **z**:

```
ge = open("great_expectations_complete.txt").read()
aardvark_count = ge.count(' aardvark ')
abacus_count = ge.count(' abacus ')
...
ziggurat_count = ge.count(' ziggurat ')
zoology_count = ge.count(' zoology ')
```

There are two problems with this approach. The first problem is that we are going to end up creating an enormous number of different variables – one for each word in the dictionary. The second problem is that the vast majority of the variables are going to store the number zero – a quick glance over the plot of *Great Expectations* should be enough to convince you that it doesn't feature any aardvarks!

In chapter 4, we learned how to use lists to store collections of data. Perhaps we can avoid creating all these variables by using a list to store the counts for all our words. Let's look at an example that just counts seven words and prints the counts :

```
ge = open("great_expectations_complete.txt").read()
words = [' aardvark ', ' abacus ', ' and ' , ' gentleman ', ' over ' ,
        ' ziggurat ', ' zoology ']❶
all_counts = []❷
for word in words:
    count = ge.count(word)
    all_counts.append(count)❸
print(all_counts)
```

print_seven_counts.py

We create a list to store the words that we want to count (this line is quite long so here it's split over two lines to make it easier to read)❶. Then, we create an empty list❷ to hold the counts. We loop over the list of words, figuring out the count for each and appending the count to the list of all counts❸.

In terms of compactness, this code is a great improvement – we have got rid of all the repetition, and if we wanted to generate counts for a much longer list of words the only thing we'd need to change is the definition of the `some_words` list[1].

If we look at the output, however, we can see a couple of problems:

```
[0, 0, 4226, 145, 163, 0, 0]
```

Although the counts are obviously being calculated, the way that they're being stored is not very useful. Once we've calculated all the counts, how do we look up the count for a given word (for example, 'gentleman')? In the original code where we had one variable per word, it would be easy:

```
print("count for gentleman is " + str(gentleman_count))
```

but because the counts are now stored under a single list, we now have to remember that 'gentleman' was the fourth word in the list before we can get the corresponding count (at index position 3, because we start counting from zero):

```
print("count for gentleman is " + str(all_counts[3]))
```

Here's the problem: the **words** and the **counts** are now disconnected – they are stored in separate variables and it's hard to go from one to the other. We can try various tricks to get round this problem. What if we used the `index()` method to figure out the position of the word we are looking for using the original list?

---

1   In a real life program, of course, we'd probably read the list of words from a separate file instead of writing it in the code.

```
i = some_words.index(' gentleman ')
print(all_counts(i))
```

This works because we have two lists of the same length, with a one-to-one correspondence between the elements:

```
print(some_words)
print(all_counts)
```

```
[' aardvark ',' abacus ',' and ',' gentleman ' ... ' zoology ']
[    0      ,    0    , 4226 ,    145        ...      0       ]
```

Using the `index()` method in this way still has major drawbacks. We need to be incredibly careful when manipulating either of the two lists to make sure that they stay perfectly synchronized – if we make any change to one list but not the other, then there will no longer be a one-to-one correspondence between elements and we'll get the wrong answer when we try to look up a count.

This approach is also slow. To find the index of a given word in the `some_words` list, Python has to look at each element one at a time until it finds the one we're looking for. This means that as the size of the word list grows, the time taken to look up the index for a given element will grow alongside it.

Finally, notice that most elements in the `all_counts` list are going to be zero (because most words don't occur at all in the text of *Great Expectations*). The more words we have in our list, the higher the proportion of zeros we are going to store.

Thinking about paired data

If we take a step back and think about this problem in more general terms, what we need is a way of storing **pairs** of data (in this case, words and their counts) in a way that allows us to efficiently look up the count for any given word. This problem of storing paired data is incredibly common in programming. We might want to store:

- words together with their counts in a big piece of text

- user names together with passwords for a login system

- the names of players together with their positions in a game

- the names of students together with their scores on a test

- your colleagues' names together with their email addresses

- the names of stocks together with their current price

- words together with their definitions

All these are examples of what we call *key-value pairs*. In each case we have pairs of *keys* and *values*:

Key	Value
word	count
user name	password
player name	player position
student	test score
name	email address
stock name	price
word	definition

The last example in this table – words and their definitions – is an interesting one because we have a tool in the physical world for storing this type of data – a dictionary. Think about how you use a physical dictionary: you start with a word, and you look up its definition. Python's tool for solving this type of problem is also called a dictionary (usually abbreviated to *dict*) and in this chapter we'll see how to create and use them.

Creating a dict

The syntax for creating a dict is similar to that for creating a list, but we use curly brackets rather than square ones. Each pair of data, consisting of a key and a value, is called an *item*. When storing items in a dict, we separate them with commas. Within an individual item, we separate the key and the value with a colon. Here's a bit of code that creates a dict of authors and their birth years with three items:

```
birth_years = { 'Charles Dickens':1812, 'Jane Austen':1775, 'Lewis
Carroll':1832 }
```

In this case, the keys are strings and the values are numbers. Splitting the dict definition over several lines and inserting some spaces makes it easier to read:

```
birth_years = {
            'Charles Dickens' : 1812,
            'Jane Austen'     : 1775,
            'Lewis Carroll'   : 1832 }
```

but doesn't affect the code at all. To retrieve a bit of data from the dict – i.e. to look up the birth year for a particular author – we write the name of the dict, followed by the key in square brackets:

```
print(birth_years['Jane Austen'])
```

The code looks very similar to using a list, but instead of giving the index of the element we want, we're giving the **key** for the **value** that we want to retrieve. Notice that this looks very different from the "two lists" approach that we sketched out earlier. When we want to retrieve a value from the dict, we **don't** have to iterate over all the items until we find the one we want – we just give the name of the key and get back the value.

Before we dive in and start learning about what we can do with dictionaries, we need to take note of a couple of restrictions. The only types of data we are allowed to use as keys are strings and numbers[1], so we can't, for example, create a dictionary where the keys are file objects. Values can be whatever type of data we like. Also, keys **must** be unique – we can't store multiple values for the same key. If we try to store the same key twice:

```
birth_years = {
            'Charles Dickens'  : 1812,
            'Jane Austen'      : 1775,
            'Lewis Carroll'    : 1832,
            'Jane Austen'      : 1776
          }
```

then the second value will just overwrite the first one.

In real life programs, it's relatively rare that we'll want to create a dict all in one go like in the example above. More often, we'll want to create an

---

1   Not strictly true; we can use any immutable type, but that is beyond the scope of this book.

empty dict, then add key/value pairs to it (just as we often create an empty list and then add elements to it).

To create an empty dict we simply write a pair of curly brackets on their own, and to add elements, we use the square brackets notation on the left hand side of an assignment. Here's a bit of code that stores the birth year data one item at a time:

```
birth_years = {}
birth_years['Charles Dickens'] = 1812
birth_years['Jane Austen'] =  1775
birth_years['Lewis Carroll'] =  1832
```

We can delete a key from a dict using the pop() method. pop() actually returns the value and deletes the key at the same time:

```
birth_years = {
                'Charles Dickens' : 1812,
                'Jane Austen'     : 1775,
                'Lewis Carroll'   : 1832 }
# remove Jane Austen from the dict
birth_years.pop('Jane Austen')
```

Counting words again

Let's take another look at the word counting example from the start of the chapter. Here's how we store the words and their counts in a dict:

```
ge = open("great_expectations_complete.txt").read()
words = [' aardvark ', ' abacus ', ' and ' , ' gentleman ', ' over ',
         ' ziggurat ', ' zoology ']
all_counts = {}❶
for word in words:
    count = ge.count(word)
    all_counts[word] = count❷
print(all_counts)
```

word_count_dict.py

The structure of this code is very similar to the earlier version which used a list. The `all_counts` variable is now a dict❶, and we add key/value pairs to the dict inside the loop❷. We can see from the output that the words and their counts are now stored together in one variable:

```
{' gentleman ': 145, ' over ': 163, ' and ': 4226, ' ziggurat ':
0, ' zoology ': 0, ' abacus ': 0, ' aardvark ': 0}
```

and if we reformat the output a bit to make it easier to read, the pairwise structure of the data becomes obvious:

```
{' gentleman ': 145,
 ' over '     : 163,
 ' and '      : 4226,
 ' ziggurat ' : 0,
 ' zoology '  : 0,
 ' abacus '   : 0,
 ' aardvark ' : 0}
```

We still have a lot of repetitive counts of zero, but looking up the count for a particular word is now very straightforward:

```
print(all_counts['gentleman'])
```

We no longer have to worry about either memorizing the order of the counts or maintaining two separate lists.

Let's now see if we can find a way of avoiding storing all those zero counts. We can add an `if` statement that ensures that we only store a count if it's greater than zero❶:

```
ge = open("great_expectations_complete.txt").read()
words = [' aardvark ', ' abacus ', ' and ' , ' gentleman ', ' over ',
         ' ziggurat ', ' zoology ']
all_counts = {}
for word in words:
    count = ge.count(word)
    if count > 0:❶
        all_counts[word] = count
print(all_counts)
```

nonzero_words.py

When we look at the output from the above code, we can see that the amount of data we're storing is much smaller – just the counts for the three words that are greater than zero:

```
{' gentleman ': 145, ' over ': 163, ' and ': 4226}
```

Now we have a new problem to deal with. Looking up the count for a given word works fine when the count is positive:

```
print(all_counts[' and '])
```

But when the count is zero, the word doesn't appear as a key in the dict:

```
print(all_counts[' aardvark '])
```

so we will get a `KeyError` when we try to look it up:

```
KeyError: ' aardvark '
```

There are two possible ways to fix this. We can check for the existence of a key in a dict (just like we can check for the existence of an element in a list), and only try to retrieve it once we know it exists:

```
if ' aardvark ' in all_counts:
    print(all_counts(' aardvark '))
```

Alternatively, we can use the dict's `get()` method. `get()` usually works just like using square brackets: the following two lines do exactly the same thing:

```
print(all_counts[' aardvark '])
print(all_counts.get(' aardvark '))
```

The thing that makes `get()` really useful, however, is that it can take an optional second argument, which is the default value to be returned if the key isn't present in the dict. In this case, we know that if a given word doesn't appear in the dict then its count is zero, so we can give zero as the default value and use `get()` to print out the count for any word:

```
print("count for gentleman is " + str(all_counts.get(' gentleman ', 0)))
print("count for aardvark is " + str(all_counts.get(' aardvark ', 0)))
print("count for zoology is " + str(all_counts.get(' zoology ', 0)))
print("count for and is " + str(all_counts.get(' and ', 0)))
```

`print_counts.py`

As we can see from the output, we now don't have to worry about whether or not any given word appears in the dict – `get()` takes care of everything and returns zero when appropriate:

179

```
count for gentleman is 145
count for aardvark is 0
count for zoology is 0
count for and is 4226
```

More generally, assuming we have a word stored in the variable word, we can run a line of code like this:

```
print("count for " + word + " is " + str(all_counts.get(word, 0)))
```

and be sure of getting the right answer.

Iterating over a dict

What if, instead of looking up a single item from a dict, we want to do something for all items? For example, imagine that we wanted to take our all_counts dict from the code above and print out all words where the count is great than 150. One way to do it would be to iterate over the list of words, looking up the count for each one and deciding whether or not to print it[1]:

```
for word in words:
    if all_counts.get(word) > 150:
        print(word)
```

As we can see from the output, this works perfectly well:

```
and
over
```

---

1 Strictly speaking, in this example there's no need to build a dict at all – we could just check the count and print a line if it's equal to two – but most programs that use dicts will be a bit more complex.

For this example, this approach works because we have a list of the words already written as part of the program. Most of the time when we create a dict, however, we'll do it using some other method which doesn't require an explicit list of the keys. Here's a more interesting version of our word counting program that uses a list of one thousand common English words stored in a file called *common_words.txt*[1]:

```
ge = open("great_expectations_complete.txt").read()
all_counts = {}

words_file = open("common_words.txt")

for line in words_file:
    word = line.rstrip("\n")❶
    count = ge.count(" " + word + " ")❷
    if count > 0:
        all_counts[word] = count
print(all_counts)
```

words_from_file.py

Notice that because this version of the code reads the words from a file, we need to remove the newline❶ and manually add spaces❷ on each side of the word.

The resulting dict has exactly the same format as in our previous examples:

```
{'all': 438, 'forget': 10, 'rob': 2, 'month': 2, 'four': 22, 'sleep':
13, 'dish': 1, 'chair': 31, 'hate': 5, 'children': 12, 'hurry': 6,
'depend': 7, 'father': 18 , ...}
```

but has many more items – 827 to be exact. Remember that we started with the thousand most common English words, so it's not surprising to

---

1   The list was taken from Wikipedia; if you want to play with this file it's in the chapter_7 examples folder.

find that around 80 percent of them occur at least once in a long book like *Great Expectations.*

Reading the words from a file, rather than writing them in the code, has allowed us to generate a much more comprehensive collection of counts. However, it means that we no longer have a handy list of all the words we counted. Now if we want to print out all the words that occurred more than 150 times, we can't simply iterate over the list of words. Instead, we need to somehow obtain the set of words directly from the dict.

Iterating over keys

When used on a dict, the keys() method returns a list of all the keys in the dict:

```
print(all_counts.keys())
```

Looking at the output[1] confirms that the keys of the dict are the words that we found at least once in the text:

```
['all', 'forget', 'rob', 'month', 'four', 'sleep', ...]
```

To find all the words that occur at least 150 times, all we have to do is take the output of keys() and iterate over it, keeping the body of the loop the same as before:

```
for word in all_counts.keys():
    if all_counts.get(word) > 150:
        print(word)
```

iterate_over_keys.py

---

1   If you're using Python 3 you might see slightly different output here, but all the code examples will work just the same

This code prints the set of set of words that occur more than 150 times in the text:

```
all
young
to
me
little
what
...
```

Before we move on, take a moment to compare the output above with the contents of the *common_words.txt* file. You'll notice that the file has the words in alphabetical order, whereas the words in the output above are not in any particular order. This illustrates an important point about dicts – they are *inherently unordered*. That means that when we use the keys() method to iterate over a dict, we can't rely on processing the items in the same order that we added them. This is in contrast to lists, which always maintain the same order when looping. If we want to control the order in which keys are printed we can use the sorted() function to sort the list of keys before processing it:

```
for word in sorted(all_counts.keys()):
    if all_counts.get(word) > 150:
        print(word)
```

```
I
a
about
after
all
...
```

Iterating over items

In the example code above, the first thing we need to do inside the loop is to look up the value for the current key. This is a very common pattern when iterating over dicts – so common, in fact, that Python has a special shorthand for it. Instead of doing this:

```
for key in my_dict.keys():
    value = my_dict.get(key)
    # do something with key and value
```

We can use the `items()` method to iterate over pairs of data, rather than just keys:

```
for key, value in my_dict.items():
    # do something with key and value
```

The `items()` method does something slightly different from all the other methods we've seen so far in this book; rather than returning a **single value**, or a **list of values**, it returns a **list of pairs of values**. That's why we have to give two variable names at the start of the loop. Here's how we can use the `items()` method to process our dict of words counts just like before:

```
for word, count in all_counts.items():
    if count > 150:
        print(word)
```

iterate_over_items.py

This approach is much more readable, and you should use it whenever you need to iterate over key/value pairs in a dict.

Lookup vs. iteration

Before we finish this chapter; a word of warning: don't make the mistake of iterating over all the items in a dict in order to look up a single value. Imagine we want to look up the number of times the word 'this' occurs in our example above. It's tempting to use the `items()` method to write a loop that looks at each item in the dict until we find the one we're looking for:

```python
for word, count in all_counts.items():
    if word == 'this':
        print(count)
```

and this will work, but it's completely unnecessary (and slow). Instead, simply use the `get()` method to ask for the value associated with the key you want:

```python
print(all_counts.get('this'))
```

Recap

We started this chapter by examining the problem of storing paired data in Python. After looking at a couple of unsatisfactory ways to do it using tools that we've already learned about, we introduced a new type of data structure – the dict – which offers a much nicer solution to the problem of storing paired data.

Later in the chapter, we saw that the real benefit of using dictionaries is the efficient lookup they provide. We saw how to create dictionaries and manipulate the items in them, and several different ways to look up values for known keys. We also saw how to iterate over all the items in a dict.

In the process, we uncovered a few restrictions on what dictionaries are capable of – we're only allowed to use a couple of different data types for keys, they must be unique, and we can't rely on their order. Just as a physical dictionary allows us to rapidly look up the definition for a word but not the other way round, Python dictionaries allow us to rapidly look up the value associated with a key, but not the reverse.

Exercises

Word counts

Imagine that we want to get an idea of what the book *Great Expectations* is about without reading it. One approach would be to simply count the number of times each word occurs in the text and print out the words that occur most frequently. Hopefully, seeing the most common words will give us a clue about the plot and content of the book.

Write a program that will read the complete text of *Great Expectations* from the file *great_expectations_complete.txt* and build a dict of word counts. Remember that the book will contain many words that aren't in the *common_words.txt* file, so you can't just reuse the code from earlier in the chapter. Use the dict to print out all the words that occur more than one thousand times in the text.

Do this exercise before looking at the next one!

Relative word frequency

You might be disappointed by the results of the previous exercise – when we print out the most common words from *Great Expectations* we just get a very boring list of common words that we might find in any book:

```
a
and
in
of
the
to
```

which will not help us to figure out what the book is about.

Thinking about the problem a bit more, what we are really interested in is the words that occur in *Great Expectations* **more frequently** than they occur in **other** books. This will filter out all the common words like "and", "or" and "the", leaving us with just the common words that are unique to *Great Expectations*.

Write a program that will build another dict of word counts for the text of the book *David Copperfield*, which is stored in the file *david_copperfield_complete.txt*. Use these two dicts to print out words that occur at least fifty times more often in *Great Expectations* than in *David Copperfield*. Remember that the two books are of different lengths!

Does this approach produce more useful words than just looking at counts? Pick two different long pieces of text and try using the same technique to print out words that occur much more frequently in one than in the other.

Solutions

Word counts

This exercise is similar to an example that we saw earlier in the chapter which generated counts for a list of common words. Let's remind ourselves of how it worked:

```
ge = open("great_expectations_complete.txt").read()
all_counts = {}

words_file = open("common_words.txt")

for line in words_file:
    word = line.rstrip("\n")
    count = ge.count(" " + word + " ")
    if count > 0:
        all_counts[word] = count
print(all_counts)
```

The main difference for this exercise is that we want to generate counts for **all** words, not just the common ones. If we had some way to create a list of all the words that are used at least once in *Great Expectations*, we could solve the problem by simply iterating over that list rather than over the common words file:

```
ge = open("great_expectations_complete.txt").read()
all_counts = {}

# somehow create a list of all words used in Great Expectations
all_words = ???

for word in all_words:
    count = ge.count(" " + word + " ")
    if count > 0:
        all_counts[word] = count
print(all_counts)
```

How might we go about creating the list `all_words`? The easiest way is to use the text itself, which we already have stored in the variable ge.

We'll start by taking the complete text and completely removing all formatting from it. We'll change it to lower case:

```
ge = ge.lower()
```

and then remove all the punctuation marks by replacing them with spaces. We could do it like this

```
ge = ge.replace(',' , '')
ge = ge.replace('.' , '')
ge = ge.replace('"' , '')
ge = ge.replace('!' , '')
...
```

but it would result in very repetitive code. Instead, we'll make a list of punctuation characters – including newlines and carriage returns – and replace them with spaces in a loop:

```
for punctuation in [',' , ':' , '.' , '"' , '!' , '?' , '-' ,
                    '(' , ')' , '\n' , '\r']:
    ge = ge.replace(punctuation, ' ')
```

What is the effect of all this manipulation on the text? If we take this sentence from near the start of the book:

```
"Hold your noise!" cried a terrible voice, as a man started up
from among the graves at the side of the church porch. "Keep
still, you little devil, or I'll cut your throat!"
```

after the text manipulation, it looks like this – all the formatting has been removed, and it's now just a string of words:

```
hold your noise cried a terrible voice as a man started up from
among the graves at the side of the church porch keep still you
little devil or i'll cut your throat
```

In order to turn this **string of words** into a **list of words**, all we have to do is to split it wherever we see a space:

```
all_words = ge.split(" ")
```

The same sentence now looks like this:

```
[ ... 'hold', 'your', 'noise', 'cried', 'a', 'terrible',
'voice', 'as', 'a', 'man', 'started', 'up', 'from', 'among',
'the', 'graves', 'at', 'the', 'side', 'of', 'the', 'church',
'porch', 'keep', 'still', 'you', 'little', 'devil', 'or',
"i'll", 'cut', 'your', 'throat' ... ]
```

and just like that we have our list of words. It's a big list – it has 188,491 elements – but it behaves just like any other list. Here's the complete code to generate the all_words list:

```
ge = open("great_expectations_complete.txt").read()
ge = ge.lower()
for punctuation in [',' , ':' , '.' , '"' , '!' , '?' , '-' ,
                    '(' , ')' , '\n' , '\r']:
    ge = ge.replace(punctuation, ' ')

all_words = ge.split(" ")
```

At this point we might be tempted to start iterating over the list of words and counting the number of times each one occurs in the text just like we've been doing before:

```
word_count = {}
for word in all_words:
    count = ge.count(' ' + word + ' ')
    word_count[word] = count
```

but there are a few problems. Firstly, our list of words is very big, so counting them all is going to be very slow. Secondly, our list is going to contain many repeated words, so we will end up counting the same word multiple times. Thirdly, we might miscount words because of punctuation – if we are counting the string " hello ", with a space on either side of the word, then we will miss out occurrences like these that involve punctuation:

```
hello!
"hello"
hello,
```

Let's consider a different approach to the problem. Rather than counting each word using the count() method, we will go through the list of words one at a time and keep a running total of the number of times we've seen each word.

To keep the running total, we'll start with an empty dict❶ to store the count data. The keys will be the words, and the values will be the counts. We'll then look at each word in turn and look up the current count (i.e. how many times we've seen this word before). If this is the first time we've seen a given word then the current count will be zero, so we'll use the get() method with a default of zero❷. We'll add one to the current count to give the new count❸, then store the new count back in the dict❹.

```
word_count = {}❶
for word in words:
    current_count = word_count.get(word, 0)❷
    new_count = current_count + 1❸
    word_count[word] = new_count❹
```

By the time we get to the end of the loop, we have seen and counted all the words, so the `word_count` dict is complete. If we print `word_count` we can see the familiar structure:

```
{ ... , 'brooches': 1, 'induced': 7, 'appearances': 2, 'hailing': 1,
'boldness': 1, 'feet': 29, 'sympathy': 5, ... }
```

The keys are all words, and the values are their counts. Now we can solve the exercise: we just iterate over the dict and, for each item, print out the word if the count is great than 1000. Here's the complete code:

```
# open and read the text
ge = open("great_expectations_complete.txt").read()

# convert the text to lower case, strip punctuation and split into words
ge = ge.lower()
for punctuation in [',' , ':' , '.' , '"' , '!' , '?' , '-' ,
                    '(' , ')' , '\n' , '\r']:
    ge = ge.replace(punctuation, ' ')
all_words = ge.split(" ")

# build up the dict of word counts
word_count = {}
for word in all_words:
    current_count = word_count.get(word, 0)
    new_count = current_count + 1
    word_count[word] = new_count

# iterate over items and print the word if the count is great than 1000
for word, count in word_count.items():
    if count > 1000:
        print(word)
```

word_counts.py

and the first few lines of output:

```
had
for
her
with
as
at
```

Relative word frequency

As the exercise description says, in order to solve this problem we need to create two dicts – one for *Great Expectations* and one for *David Copperfield*. As we saw in chapter 5, when we need to run the same code multiple times it's a good idea to turn it into a function, so let's start by taking our code from the previous exercise and making a function. The function will take one argument – a string containing text – and will return a dict containing the word counts:

```
def build_word_count_dict(text):
    text = text.lower()
    for punctuation in [',' , ':' , '.' , '"' , '!' , '?' , '-' ,
                        '(' , ')' , '\n' , '\r']:
        text = text.replace(punctuation, ' ')

    all_words = text.split(" ")

    word_count = {}
    for word in all_words:
        current_count = word_count.get(word, 0)
        new_count = current_count + 1
        word_count[word] = new_count

    return word_count
```

Notice how the code that removes the formatting, splits the text, and builds the dict is exactly the same as before – all we have added is the function definition and the return line. Building our two dicts is now quite straightforward – we just read the text from the appropriate files, call our new function, and store the results in variables:

```
ge_text = open("great_expectations_complete.txt").read()
ge_word_counts = build_word_count_dict(ge_text)

dc_text = open("david_copperfield_complete.txt").read()
dc_word_counts = build_word_count_dict(dc_text)
```

Next, we can move on to the problem of finding words that occur more often in *Great Expectations* than in *David Copperfield*. For each word in the ge_word_counts dict, we would like to look up the count for the same word in the dc_word_counts dict:

```
for word, ge_count in ge_word_counts.items():
    dc_count = dc_word_counts.get(word)
```

We're looking for words that occur at least fifty times more often in *Great Expectations* than in *David Copperfield*, so it's tempting to just test if ge_count is more than fifty times greater than dc_count❶:

```
for word, ge_count in ge_word_counts.items():
    dc_count = dc_word_counts.get(word)
    if ge_count > dc_count * 50:❶
        print(word)
```

but this fails to take into account the fact that the books are different lengths. *Great Expectations* is about 189,000 words, whereas *David Copperfield* is about 363,000 words. In order to properly compare the two counts, we need to convert them into **frequencies** – rather than looking at how many times a word occurs, we need to look at how many times it occurs per million words[1].

---

1   Or per thousand words, or per ten words – the exact units don't matter as long as they are

At this point, we need a bit of simple maths. If we know the number of times a word occurs in *Great Expectations*, we can calculate its frequency per million words by dividing the count by the length of the text (189,000 words) then multiplying by 1,000,000:

```
ge_frequency = (ge_count / 189,000) * 1,000,000
```

and we can do the same for *David Copperfield* but with the different length:

```
dc_frequency = (dc_count / 363,000) * 1,000,000
```

We could just put these calculations inside the loop:

```
for word, ge_count in ge_word_counts.items():
    dc_count = dc_word_counts.get(word)

    ge_frequency = (ge_count / 189,000) * 1,000,000
    dc_frequency = (dc_count / 363,000) * 1,000,000

    if ge_frequency > dc_frequency * 50:
        print(word)
```

but a more elegant solution might be to change our function so that instead of returning a dict of counts, it returns a dict of frequencies:

---

consistent.

196

```
from __future__ import division

def build_word_freq_dict(text):
    text = text.lower()
    for punctuation in [',' , ':' , '.' , '"' , '!' , '?' , '-' ,
                        '(' , ')' , '\n' , '\r']:
        text = text.replace(punctuation, ' ')
    all_words = text.split(" ")

    word_count = {}
    for word in all_words:
        current_count = word_count.get(word, 0)
        new_count = current_count + 1
        word_count[word] = new_count

    word_frequency = {}
    for word, count in word_count.items(): ❶
        freq = (count / len(all_words)) * 1000000
        word_frequency[word] = freq

    return word_frequency
```

All we've done here is add a second step❶ that builds a word frequency dict by carrying out the frequency calculation for each word in the word_count dict. If we now change our function calls to use the new function:

```
ge_text = open("great_expectations_complete.txt").read()
ge_word_freqs = build_word_freq_dict(ge_text)

dc_text = open("david_copperfield_complete.txt").read()
dc_word_freqs = build_word_freq_dict(dc_text)
```

then we can write our loop to iterate over each word and compare the frequencies:

```
for word, ge_freq in ge_word_freqs.items():
    dc_freq = dc_word_freqs[word]
    if ge_freq > dc_freq * 50:
        print(word)
```

Unfortunately, this code runs into trouble as soon as we encounter a word that appears in *Great Expectations* but not in *David Copperfield*:

```
    dc_freq = dc_word_freqs[word]
KeyError: 'aided'
```

Remember that the dc_word_freqs dict only contains frequencies for words that appear at least once in *David Copperfield*. When we try to look up the count for a word that doesn't appear at all – in this case, 'aided' – we get a KeyError.

We learned the solution to this problem earlier in the chapter – use the get() method and supply a sensible default❶. We might think that the default value should be zero:

```
for word, ge_freq in ge_word_freqs.items():
    dc_freq = dc_word_freqs.get(word, 0)❶
    if ge_freq > dc_freq * 50:
        print(word)
```

but the problem with this approach is that it will print out **all** words that **don't** appear in *David Copperfield*, even if they occur only once in *Great Expectations* (zero times ten is still zero, so as long as the ge_freq is greater than zero the word will be printed).

Picking a default frequency for words that aren't in *David Copperfield* is really more of a philosophical question than a programming one. Essentially it's asking: if Charles Dickens kept on adding chapters to *David Copperfield* until it was infinitely long, what would the frequency of the word be? This is obviously impossible to answer, so for now, let's use a frequency of 1 as the default[1]. Here's the final code:

---

1   Remember that this is 1 per million words, so still very infrequent.

```
from __future__ import division

def build_word_freq_dict(text):
    text = text.lower()
    for punctuation in [',', ':', '.','"', '!', '?', '--','(', ')',
                        '\n', '\r']:
        text = text.replace(punctuation, ' ')
    all_words = text.split(" ")

    word_count = {}
    for word in all_words:
        current_count = word_count.get(word, 0)
        new_count = current_count + 1
        word_count[word] = new_count

    word_frequency = {}
    for word, count in word_count.items():
        freq = (count / len(all_words)) * 1000000
        word_frequency[word] = freq

    return word_frequency

# build the frequency dict for Great Expectations
ge_text = open("great_expectations_complete.txt").read()
ge_word_freqs = build_word_freq_dict(ge_text)

# build the frequency dict for David Copperfield
dc_text = open("david_copperfield_complete.txt").read()
dc_word_freqs = build_word_freq_dict(dc_text)

# iterate over words in Great Expectations and print them
for word, ge_freq in ge_word_freqs.items():
    dc_freq = dc_word_freqs.get(word, 1)
    if ge_freq > dc_freq * 50:
        print(word)
```

`word_frequencies.py`

When we finally run the code, we get a much more interesting set of words than we got in the first exercise. Some are names of characters:

```
jaggers
havisham
herbert
estella
pip
```

some are place names (all in London):

```
hammersmith
newgate
richmond
```

and some are descriptions of settings and people:

```
steamer
sergeant
forge
blacksmith
marshes
convict
parlor
```

Just for fun, we can easily do the exercise the other way round – which words are at least fifty times more frequent in *David Copperfield* than in *Great Expectations*?

```
for word, dc_freq in dc_word_freqs.items():
    ge_freq = ge_word_freqs.get(word, 1)
    if dc_freq > ge_freq * 50:
        print(word)
```

Just as before, we get a mixture of characters:

```
uriah
dora
david
micawber
```

places:

```
highgate
canterbury
```

and settings and people:

```
downstairs
drawing-room
mills
aunt
doctor
honour
parlour
```

Interestingly, the word 'parlour' occurs in both lists, but with different spellings – in the versions of the texts we are using, *Great Expectations* uses American English ('parlor') whereas *David Copperfield* uses UK English ('parlour').

What have we learned?

What we have implemented here is a well known technique for text mining. The process of splitting up a piece of text into words is often called *tokenization* and the process of comparing the frequencies is called *frequency analysis*. Variations on this technique can be used to investigate all sorts of text. For example, we could compare word frequencies in speeches by two rival politicians to figure out which issues they each think is more important. Or we could compare word frequencies in newspapers from today and from fifty years ago, to see how the topics have changed.

In more general terms, the techniques used in these exercises will be useful for any program that relies on being able to look up a piece of information. In our example, we are looking up the frequency for a given word. The same approach will be useful when looking up the health of a player in a video game, looking up the price of a stock on a particular date, or looking up a user's preferences for a web application.

▌8: Modules, objects and classes

Introduction

One of the reason that Python is so often recommended as a first programming language is that it has lots of useful functions and methods built in to the language. In this book we've looked at tools for manipulating strings and numbers, for reading and writing files, and for storing data in various ways. These functions and data types are likely to be needed in pretty much every program and as such, they are always available. If we want to open a file, we simply write a statement that uses the open() function.

However, there's another category of tools in Python which are more specialized – tools which are very useful when you need them, but are not likely to be needed for the majority of programs. Examples include tools for doing advanced mathematical calculations, for downloading data from the web, for running external programs, and for manipulating dates. Each collection of specialized tools – really just a collection of specialized **functions** and **data types** – is called a *module*.

The idea of modules is certainly not unique to Python – pretty much all programming languages have something similar (sometimes they are called *libraries* rather than *modules*, but they do the same job). However, Python stands out because it comes with a large collection of useful modules which you can very easily use in your programs. These modules – which together we call the **Python Standard Library** – are designed to solve common programming problems, and by taking advantage of them, we can often write programs more more quickly and be confident that they will run reliably.

In this chapter, we're going to look at how to use modules and take a brief tour of some of the most commonly used ones. There are hundreds of modules in the Python Standard Library, each of which could easily be the topic for an entire chapter, so we won't be able to look at any of them in detail. However, this chapter should give you the background to be able to find and use the modules that you need.

Using modules

For reasons of efficiency, Python doesn't automatically make every module available in each new program, as it does with the more basic tools. Instead, we have to explicitly load each module that we want to use inside our program. To load a module we use the `import` statement. For example, the module that deals with dates and times is called `datetime`, so in order to use it we have to include the line:

```
import datetime
```

at the start of our program.

The `datetime` module is a great example to look at, because it allows us to do all sorts of things that would be difficult and error prone if we tried to write all the code ourselves. Consider a very simple example: figuring out my age in days. There are six pieces of information involved: the year, month, and day when I was born, and the year, month, and day of today:

```
# I was born on 27th May 1981
birth_year = 1981
birth_month = 5
birth_day = 27

# today is 11th June 2015
current_year = 2015
current_month = 6
current_day = 11
```

How would we start the calculation? We could begin by taking the difference between the years and multiplying by 365 – but what about leap years, which are a day longer? Then we could add the difference between months – but some months have 30 days and some have 31 days, except for February, which has 28 days, unless **this** year is a leap year in which case it has 29. It's easy to imagine how complicated the code will get if we try to apply these rules.

However, if we use the datetime module, the problem becomes easy. First we create a new date object to store my date of birth. A date object is a bit like a file object – it's designed to store a particular type of data, and has useful methods for manipulating that data. The function that creates a new date object is simply called date(), and it takes three arguments – the year, month and day. Because the date() function is part of the datetime module, we have to use the module name as part of the function call. We write the name of the module, then a period, then the name of the function (with arguments in parentheses as normal):

```
birthday = datetime.date(1981, 5, 27)
```

If we try to print the birthday variable, it will display the date in a standard format:

```
1981-05-27
```

This looks like the simple string "1981-05-27", but don't be fooled – what we're seeing is just a **representation** of the variable `birthday`.

Next, we need to create another `date` object to store today's date. We could use the same function call as before and just replace the numbers:

```
now = datetime.date(2015, 6, 11)
```

but that would mean that if I ran the program tomorrow, it would give the wrong answer. Instead, there's a special method to create a `date` object to store today's date:

```
now = datetime.date.today()
```

Notice how we call the method. The name of the method is `today()`, and it lives inside the `date` object, which lives inside the `datetime` module, so we have to use all three names. If we print out the `now` variable, we'll get a representation of the date just like before:

```
2015-06-11
```

but it'll be different depending on when we run the program.

The final step is to calculate the difference between the dates. Thanks to the way that `date` objects are designed, we can just use the minus symbol to subtract the birth date from today's date:

```
age = now - birthday
```

The result of subtracting one date from another is a new type of object: a `timedelta` object. This is another specialized data type that is designed to store **differences** between dates and times. When we print out the age variable, it prints a representation of the difference:

```
12433 days, 0:00:00
```

and we have our answer – at the time I'm writing this chapter, I'm 12,433 days old. The complete code is extremely brief:

```
import datetime
birthday = datetime.date(1981, 5, 27)
now = datetime.date.today()
age = now - birthday
print(age)
```

age_in_days.py

when we consider all the complex calculations that are going on. That's because all of the complex calculations are hidden inside the `datetime` module – somebody else has already written all that code, so we don't have to.

Classes and objects

So far in this book we've encountered several different data types. We started off with **strings**, which were easy to understand: a string object stores a single bit of data and has some useful methods for manipulating it. We then encountered **file objects**, which are a little more complicated: a file object represents a file on disk (we might want to say that it stores the path to the file, or the file name) and offers access to the file contents via methods. Later on we learned about two different data types for storing collections of things: **lists** and **dicts**, which also have methods for manipulating and retrieving data. And just recently we looked at **date** and **timedelta** objects, which store date and time information and have methods for manipulating them.

To understand how all these data types work together, we need to go into a bit more detail. All of the data types mentioned above are examples of *classes*. A class is just a way of bundling together some data and some methods that use that data. When we say that Python has a string class, we simply mean that somewhere in the Python language is a definition of an object that has a piece of data (a string of characters) and some methods (`lower()`, `replace()`, `count()`, etc.) that can operate on that data. When we create a string in Python:

```
name = "Martin"
```

we create an *instance* of the class. The actual name of the string class in Python is `str`. Every string instance has the same methods, but stores a different string of characters.

Similarly, when we say that the `datetime` module allows us to create `date` objects, what we really mean is that the module contains a definition of a `date` class. The `date` class defines a type of object that stores three numbers – a year, a month, and a day – along with some useful methods for manipulating those numbers. When we create a date object:

```
birthday = datetime.date(1981, 5, 27)
```

we are really telling Python to create a new instance of the `date` class with those particular values for the year, month and day. Just like with strings, all date objects have the same methods, but can have different values for the year, month and day.

In order to be able to use the specialized classes that are provided by modules, we don't need to know any of the details about how classes are actually defined or built. It is important, however, that we understand these three ideas:

Every value in Python is an instance of a class

Whenever we create a new value in Python, we create a new instance of a class:

```
name = "Martin" #create a new string instance
number = 42 # create a new integer instance
my_file = open("file.txt") # create a new file instance
my_list = [1,2,3] # create a new list instance
birthday = datetime.date(1981, 5, 27) # create a new date instance
```

Some classes, like strings and numbers, are often used directly:

```
print("Hello "+ name)
big_number = 100000 + number
```

Others, like files and dates, are nearly always used by calling methods on them[1]:

```
text = my_file.read()
day_of_the_week = birthday.weekday()
```

Classes like lists are in between: sometimes we use them directly[2]:

---

[1] The datetime example we saw earlier, where we used the minus symbol, is a bit of an exception.

[2] In fact, even when we use a value directly like this it actually works by calling a method behind the scenes, but we don't need to worry about that at this stage.

```
big_list = my_list + [4,5,6]
for number in big_list:
    # do something with number
```

and other times we call methods on them:

```
my_list.append(7)
my_list.reverse()
```

The class of an object determines what we can do with it

This is an idea that we encountered right at the start of the book – we can convert a string to upper case, but not a number:

```
name = "Martin"
print(name.upper()) #OK
number = 42
print(number.upper()) #Error
```

and we can divide a number, but not a string:

```
print(35 / 5) # OK
print('Hello' / 5) # Error
```

Sometimes the rules get a little complicated: for example, we can get the length of a string or a list in the same way:

```
print(len('Hello'))
print(len([3,1,4,1,5]))
```

but when we're talking about methods, they only work on the right type of object.

There can be several different ways to create an instance of a class

We have encountered this idea before, though we've not mentioned it explicitly. For example, look at the different ways we can create an instance of the string class:

```
# by writing a string literal
my_string = "Hello"

# by concatenating two strings
greeting = my_string + " world"

# by calling a method on a different string
personal_greeting = greeting.replace('world', 'Martin')

# by using the str() function on a number
number_string = str(42)

# by reading the contents of a file
file_contents = open("my_file.txt").read()
```

The important thing to remember is that all of these strings, once they've been created, behave in exactly the same way – they have the same set of methods and they are instances of the same class.

The same applies to the date class we looked at above. We saw how we can create a date object by giving a specific year, month and day:

```
birthday = datetime.date(1981, 5, 27)
```

or by using a special method that will create a date with the current year, month and day:

```
now = datetime.date.today()
```

Many of the classes that are supplied by the modules in the Python Standard Library can be created using several different methods. Methods that create objects like this are often called *constructors*.

Finding out about classes and modules

These three important facts about classes yield three important questions. How do we find out what modules are available to help with a given problem? How do we find out what classes a given module supplies? And how do we find out what constructors and methods are available for a given class?

The answers to all three lie in the excellent documentation for the Python Standard Library. The overview page is probably the single most important URL when you're learning Python[1]:

```
https://docs.python.org/2/library/index.html
```

This page gives single line descriptions of the various modules and will help you figure out which ones are likely to be useful for your specific problem. Clicking on the name of a module will take you to the documentation page for that module – here's the page for the datetime module:

```
https://docs.python.org/2/library/datetime.html
```

At the top of each module page is a brief overview of the types of problem that it's designed to solve. The menu on the left lists the different data types that are part of the module: clicking on the name of one of the data types will bring you to the detailed documentation for that data type. This

---

1   If you're using Python 3 it's `https://docs.python.org/3.3/library/index.html`

is where you'll find instructions for creating objects, and lists of useful methods.

Many modules contain multiple data types that are designed to work together (for example, `date` and `timedelta` from our `datetime` example above) so it's well worth reading the complete documentation for any module you're thinking of using. The module pages often contain useful example code that illustrates how the various data types can be used.

The standard data types that are not part of modules – strings, numbers, file objects, lists, etc. – have their own documentation:

https://docs.python.org/2/library/stdtypes.html

If you browse the section of the page that deals with strings, for example, you'll find all the familiar methods like `count()`, `endswith()` and `rstrip()` along with many other useful methods like `translate()`, `swapcase()` and `join()`. You'll also find documentation for standard data types that we've not discussed – things like `set` objects, which are used for storing collections of unique values.

Some useful modules

collections

The `collections` module[1] contains data types for storing data in special scenarios. Of particular interest to us is the `Counter` data type, which is designed to take a list of things and count the number of times each thing occurs – exactly the problem that we were solving in the word count

---

1   https://docs.python.org/2/library/collections.html

exercise at the end of chapter 7. To use a `Counter`, we call the counter constructor with the list of things as an argument:

```
import collections
cnt = collections.Counter(['a', 'b', 'a', 'c', 'a', 'c', 'd'])
```

This builds a dict where the keys are the things (in this case, single letter strings), and the values are their counts. We can use the `Counter` just like a dict to look up the count for a given string:

```
print(cnt['a']) # prints 3
```

but it also has a special method which returns the ten (or any number) most common elements along with their counts:

```
print(cnt.most_common(10))
```

Using `collections.Counter`, we could rewrite our answer to the first exercise from chapter 7 (printing the most common words in a long text) like this:

```
import collections

# read the text and turn it into a list of words
text = open("great_expectations_complete.txt").read()
text = text.lower()
for punctuation in [',', ':', '.','"', '!', '?', '--','(', ')', '\n',
'\r']:
    text = text.replace(punctuation, ' ')
all_words = text.split(" ")

cnt = collections.Counter(all_words)
print(cnt.most_common(10))
```

counter.py

This is an improvement over our original solution – not only is the code more concise, but it gives us the words sorted by frequency:

```
[('', 40352), ('the', 8143), ('and', 7071), ('i', 6466), ('to', 5075),
('of', 4431), ('a', 4040), ('in', 3024), ('that', 2978), ('was', 2829)]
```

math

We've already seen how basic mathematical operations like addition and subtraction are built into Python. However, there's a large collection of other useful mathematical processes which live in the `math` module[1]. There are functions for powers and logarithms:

```python
import math
print(math.exp(5)) # print e to the power 5
print(math.log(12345)) # print the log of 12345
print(math.pow(10,20)) # print 10 raised to the power 20
print(math.sqrt(555)) # print the square root of 555
```

math.py

functions for trigonometry:

```python
print(math.cos(1.5)) # print the cos of 1.5 radians
```

and some useful constants. Constants are simply variables that live inside modules: in `math` we have **pi** (`math.pi`) and **e** (`math.e`).

The `math` module is interesting because, unlike `datetime` or `collections`, it doesn't actually provide any new data types – it just contains useful functions.

---

1   https://docs.python.org/2/library/math.html

fractions

Staying in the world of numbers, we have the `fractions` module[1] which allow us to work with fractional numbers. We can create a new fractional number by giving a numerator and a denominator (which are just fancy words for the number on the top and the bottom):

```
f = fractions.Fraction(1,3) # create a fraction of one third
```

or we can write our fraction as a string and let Python figure it out:

```
f = fractions.Fraction('1/3') # create a fraction of one third
```

Once we've created a fraction, we can use addition, multiplication etc. as normal:

```
# what is two thirds multiplied by one sixth?
print(fractions.Fraction('2/3') * fractions.Fraction('1/6'))
```

and we get the answer expressed as a fraction:

```
Fraction(1, 9)
```

random

All of the programs we've written in this book have been completely deterministic – in other words, they behave exactly the same every time we run them. However, for many real world problems we want to introduce some random behaviour, and the `random` module[2] contains

---

1   https://docs.python.org/2/library/fractions.html
2   https://docs.python.org/2/library/random.html

functions that allow us to do so. We can pick a random number between one and ten:

```
print(random.randint(1,10))
```

shuffle a list into a random order:

```
my_list = [1,2,3,4,5,6,7,8,9]
random.shuffle(my_list)
```

or pick a random element from a list:

```
print(random.choice(my_list))
```

Random numbers turn out to be particularly useful when creating games.

os and shutil

These two modules are often grouped together because they do similar things: move, copy, rename, delete, and generally manipulate files and folders. In general, the functions inside os[1] are useful for manipulating individual files:

```
os.mkdir("new_folder") # create a new folder
os.rename("old_file.txt", "new_file.txt") # rename a file
os.remove("my_file.txt") # delete a file
```

whereas functions inside shutil[2] are useful for manipulating folders full of data:

---

1   https://docs.python.org/2/library/os.html
2   https://docs.python.org/2/library/shutil.html

```
shutil.copytree("old", "new") # copy the folder and all its contents
shutil.rmtree("my_folder") # delete the folder and all its contents
```

There is much more that the os module can do, but much of it is related to specific operating systems so we won't cover it here.

email

As you can probably guess from the name, the email module[1] contains functions and data types for sending and receiving email. This is a complex process, and the module is split up into several sub-modules. If we look at a piece of example code which sends an email:

```
import smtplib
import email.mime.text

fp = open(textfile, 'rb')
msg = email.mime.text.MIMEText(fp.read())
fp.close()


msg['Subject'] = 'Hi from Martin'
msg['From'] = martin@example.com
msg['To'] = dave@example.com

s = smtplib.SMTP('localhost')
s.sendmail(me, [you], msg.as_string())
s.quit()
```

we can see how a lot of the complexity arises: there are many bits of information – the addresses, the subject, the server name – that need to be managed.

---

1   https://docs.python.org/2/library/email.html

csv

Here's another module that would have been very useful when we were working on the exercises: specifically, the exercise where we had to read a comma separated values file in chapter 6. Because this is such a common and useful file format, there's a module specifically designed to read and write it. Using the csv module[1], we could start our solution to the chapter 6 exercise like this:

```
import csv
data = open("data.csv")
data_reader = csv.reader(data)
for row in data_reader:
    title = row[0]
    year = int(row[1])
    type = row[2]
    length = row[3]
    print(title + " published in " + str(year))
```

csv.py

The csv reader object will take care of processing the file line by line, splitting each line up into columns, and can also handle different delimiters and other formatting options.

Non standard modules

The Python Standard Library is an excellent resource when you're writing programs to solve problems in the real word. The modules are reliable, well designed, and have excellent documentation. Because they're included when you install Python, you don't have to do anything special to start using them, and if you give a copy of your program to somebody else, you can be confident that they'll be able to run it, because they will also have the modules they need.

---

1   https://docs.python.org/2/library/csv.html

However, sometimes you need to solve a very specific type of problem for which there is no suitable module in the standard library. Happily, Python also has a large collection of non standard modules – modules that are not part of the standard library, and therefore are not bundled together with Python.

Using one of these non standard modules requires a bit more work, because you have to install the module separately. Usually this is not too difficult; Python has built in tools to make installing modules easy and most non standard modules have installation instructions on their website.

While there are hundreds of modules in the standard library, there are many thousand of non standard modules, so it's impossible to list them all. There are modules for creating games[1], for doing image manipulation[2], for building web applications[3], and for drawing charts[4] – in fact, for solving nearly any conceivable problem.

Recap

We started this chapter by looking at one particular module – `datetime` – and seeing how it helps us to solve problems involving dates. In order to explain the behaviour of the new data types we encountered, we have to examine the way that data types work in a little bit more detail. Doing so helped to explain some examples of the way that data types behave from previous chapters.

---

1   http://www.pygame.org/wiki/about
2   http://www.pythonware.com/products/pil/
3   http://flask.pocoo.org/
4   http://matplotlib.org/

Next, we saw how to go about finding useful modules in Python's Standard Library, and learned that the documentation can also be useful for getting more detail on data types that we already know about.

We finished the chapter with a very brief tour of some commonly used modules. It's not necessary – and probably impossible – to memorize the modules and data types that we mentioned, but it's useful to know that they exist and that you can find out more information when you need them.

Exercises

Birthday day

Use the `datetime` module to figure out what day of the week your one hundredth birthday falls on. How about your 50th birthday? How about your 78th?

You'll have to take a look at the `datetime` documentation to help you!

Dealing cards

Write a program that will simulate shuffling a deck of cards and then dealing out a hand of five cards. If you deal one thousand five-card hands, how many of them would you expect to have all five cards of the same suit?

Solutions

Birthday day

We can use datetime to answer the first part of the question very easily. We already know how to construct a date object to represent a particular date, and it's straightforward to figure out the date of my hundredth birthday – we just add 100 to the year, bringing it from 1981 to 2081. We can create a date object:

```
import datetime

hundredth_birthday = datetime.date(2081, 5, 27)
print(hundredth_birthday)
```

and when we print out the object to check, everything looks OK:

```
2081-05-27
```

Now to figure out the day of the week. A quick look at the documentation page for datetime reveals two date object methods that look like they might be useful: weekday() and isoweekday(). If read the documentation we can see that they both return a number to represent the day of the week; the only difference is that weekday() goes from 0 to 6 to represent Monday to Sunday, whereas isoweekday() goes from 1 to 7.

Let's go with weekday() for now. Calling the method and printing the result:

```
print(hundredth_birthday.weekday())
```

gives us the output:

```
1
```

which we can easily translate to a Tuesday (since Monday is represented by zero).

So far, so good. But as the question indicates, what we'd really like is to be able to do is pick **any** birthday number, and figure out the day of the week. The simplest solution is to make the birthday number a variable, and add it to the birth year before constructing the `date` object:

```
import datetime

birthday_number = 65
birthday_year = 1981 + birthday_number

birthday = datetime.date(birthday_year, 5, 27)
print(birthday.weekday())
```

If we want to be a bit more explicit, we could use the date `replace()` method, which lets us take an existing date and alter the year, month or day:

```
import datetime

birthday_number = 65

date_of_birth = datetime.date(1981, 5, 27)

# the year we are looking for is year of birth plus the birthday number
birthday_year = date_of_birth.year + birthday_number

# take the birthday and replace the year with the year we're looking for
birthday = date_of_birth.replace(year=birthday_year)
print(birthday.weekday())
```

But that is probably a bit too complicated for a simple problem like this.

Incidentally, it might be tempting to use a `timedelta` object to simply add the number of years to the date of birth like this:

```
import datetime

birthday_number = 65

date_of_birth = datetime.date(1981, 5, 27)

one_year = datetime.timedelta(days=365) # object to represent one year
birthday = date_of_birth + (one_year * birthday_number)
```

but this will give us the wrong answer – leap years are not exactly 365 days long, so if we print out the `birthday` variable we get the output:

```
2046-05-11
```

The year is correct, but the day has drifted from 27 to 11. This illustrates just how easy it is to make mistakes when dealing with dates!

Finally, in order to make the program more user friendly, it would be good to print the actual day of the week rather than the number which represents it. Looking up the day of the week for a given number is a problem that's easily solved using a dict. Here's the final code – you'll obviously have to change the definition of `birthday_year` and `birthday` to get the correct result for your own birthday.

```
import datetime

days_of_week = {0 : 'Monday',
                1 : 'Tuesday',
                2 : 'Wednesday',
                3 : 'Thursday',
                4 : 'Friday',
                5 : 'Saturday',
                6 : 'Sunday'}

birthday_number = 65
birthday_year = 1981 + birthday_number

birthday = datetime.date(birthday_year, 5, 27)
print(days_of_week[birthday.weekday()])
```

birthday_day.py

Dealing cards

There are several parts to this problem. Firstly, how do we represent a deck of cards? Secondly, how do we pick five random cards from a deck? Thirdly, how do we repeat this process many times?

Let's start with the first problem. There are many different ways to tackle it, but this simplest is just to use strings to represent the different playing cards. We can come up with a simple scheme where each card is described by two characters – a number or J/Q/K to represent the value and a letter to represent the suit (H, D, S and C for hearts, diamonds, spades and clubs). So "7H" represents the seven of hearts, "QS" represents the queen of spades, etc.

We can represent a deck of cards by just making a list of these strings. One option is to write all the cards out manually:

```
deck = ['1H' , '2H' , '3H', ...]
```

but a better way is to use two loops to generate all the different cards:

```
values = [1,2,3,4,5,6,7,8,9,10, 'J', 'Q', 'K']❶
suits = ['H', 'D', 'S', 'C']❷
deck = []
for value in values:
    for suit in suits:
        card = str(value) + suit❸
        deck.append(card)❹
print(deck)
```

In this bit of code, we define a list to hold the 13 different values❶ and the 4 different suits❷. We create an empty list to hold the cards, then use two nested for loops to match up each possible value with each possible suit. We create each card by simply concatenating the value and suit❸, then add it to the deck❹. Notice that because some of the values are numbers and some are strings, we need to use the str() function to turn the value into a string before we can use it in a concatenation. We print the deck list at the end so we can see the result:

```
['1H', '1D', '1S', '1C', '2H', '2D', '2S', '2C', '3H', '3D', '3S', '3C',
 '4H', '4D', '4S', '4C', '5H', '5D', '5S', '5C', '6H', '6D', '6S', '6C',
 '7H', '7D', '7S', '7C', '8H', '8D', '8S', '8C', '9H', '9D', '9S', '9C',
 '10H', '10D', '10S', '10C', 'JH', 'JD', 'JS', 'JC', 'QH', 'QD', 'QS',
 'QC', 'KH', 'KD', 'KS', 'KC']
```

Take a moment to look at the output and make sure you understand where all these strings have come from, and why all the aces are first, then the twos, etc. – it's because we loop over the values first, then the suits.

Now we have our deck of cards, we come to the problem of shuffling them. Shuffling cards is a random process, so it's the random module which is going to help us. A look at the documentation tells us that the random module actually has a method called shuffle(). Let's try using it and see what the effect is:

```
random.shuffle(deck)
print(deck)
```

As expected, the elements of the deck list are now in a random order (the output will be different each time we run the program):

```
['9C', '7H', '4S', 'QD', '3C', '1C', '4C', '9D', '5C', '5H', '8H', 'JD',
'KS', '9H', 'KD', 'KC', '10S', '7D', '8C', '1H', '1D', 'JC', '2S', '4D',
'2C', '8S', '6C', '5S', '3H', '3D', '3S', '6S', 'QH', '6D', '10D', '7C',
'QC', '2H', 'QS', '10C', '2D', '9S', '1S', 'JS', '10H', 'JH', '6H',
'8D', '5D', '4H', '7S', 'KH']
```

Dealing a hand of five cards is now as simple as taking the first five elements of the deck list:

```
hand = deck[0:5]
print(hand)
```

```
['9C', '7H', '4S', 'QD', '3C']
```

In this case, we get the nine of clubs, the seven of hearts, the four of spades, the queen of diamonds and the three of clubs.

Given a list of five cards like this, how can we tell if they are all the same suit? We need to examine the second character of each string and check if they're all the same. We could write something like this:

```
card1 = hand[0] # get the first card in the hand
card1_suit = card1[1] # get the second character of the card
card2 = hand[1] # get the second card in the hand
card2_suit = card2[1] # get the second character of the card
...

if card1_suit == card2_suit and
   card2_suit == card3_suit and
   card3_suit == card4_suit and
   card4_suit == card5_suit:
    print("all suits are the same!")
```

but this would be very repetitive. Instead, let's try this idea: start by looking at the suit of the first card and storing it in a variable❶ . Then look at the suits for all the cards in turn❷. As soon as we see a card whose suit is not equal to the one we stored, we know that the cards are **not** all the same suit:

```
first_card = hand[0]
first_card_suit = first_card[1]❶
for card in hand:❷
    if card[1] != first_card_suit:
        print("cards are not all the same suit!")
```

The above code gives the idea, but it becomes clearer if we write it as a function. The function will take a hand of five cards as the argument, and return True if they all have the same suit and False if they don't:

```
def same_suit(hand):
    first_card = hand[0]
    first_card_suit = first_card[1]
    for card in hand:
        if card[1] != first_card_suit:❶
            return False
    return True❷
```

The logic of this function is a little complicated, because there are two places that the function can return. If we see a card that has a different suit to the first card, then we can return False right away❶. But if we reach the end of the loop and we haven't returned, then we know that none of the cards have had a different suit to the first one, so we can return True❷.

Here's a version of the code that will generate a random hand each time the program is run and print it out. If the cards in the hand are all the same suit, it will also print out a message:

```python
import random

# function to test if all cards in a list have the same suit
def same_suit(hand):
    first_card = hand[0]
    first_card_suit = first_card[1]
    for card in hand:
        if card[1] != first_card_suit:
            return False
    return True

# construct the deck by matching each value with each suit
values = [1,2,3,4,5,6,7,8,9,10, 'J', 'Q', 'K']
suits = ['H', 'D', 'S', 'C']
deck = []
for value in values:
    for suit in suits:
        card = str(value) + suit
        deck.append(card)

# shuffle the deck
random.shuffle(deck)

# pick a hand of five cards and check if they're all the same suit
hand = deck[0:5]
print(hand)
if same_suit(hand):
    print("all cards are the same suit")
```

Try running this program – you'll probably have to run it many times
before you happen to get a hand with all the same suit:

```
...
['KD', '4H', '3S', '1D', 'QC']
['4C', 'JH', '1S', 'QC', '8D']
['9D', 'JD', '3D', '10D', '10D']
 all cards are the same suit
['3D', 'KD', '10S', 'KH', 'JD']
...
```

Now we have a system in place for picking hands and checking suits, we
can start to address the final question: if we do this one thousand times,
how many same-suit hands will we get? We'll create a new variable❶ to
hold the number of same-suit hands we've seen, then use range()❷ to
write a loop that will run 1000 times. Each time round the loop we'll
shuffle the deck, take the first five cards, and increase the same-suit count
by one if they all have the same suit❸:

```
same_suit_hands = 0❶
for i in range(1000):❷
    random.shuffle(deck)
    hand = deck[0:5]
    if same_suit(hand):
        same_suit_hands = same_suit_hands + 1❸
print(same_suit_hands)
```

cards.py

Notice that the code which creates the deck is not inside the loop – we
only have to create the deck once. The program produces just a single
number as the output, which is the number of same-suit hands. It'll be
different each time you run the program, but most of the time it's either
one or two hands out of a thousand.

If we want to get a more accurate measurement, we can just change the number in the loop to run a million hands:

```
for i in range(1000000):
    ...
```

The program will take a lot longer to run, but will generate more accurate results – the answer is normally around 1200 hands per million. Finally, we can see what effect changing the hand size has: how many same-suit hands do we expect if we deal six cards❶ rather than five?

```
same_suit_hands = 0
for i in range(1000000):
    random.shuffle(deck)
    hand = deck[0:6]  ❶
    if same_suit(hand):
        same_suit_hands = same_suit_hands + 1
print(same_suit_hands)
```

The answer is just 175 hands out of a million.

Afterword

This is the end of *Python for Complete Beginners*; I hope you have enjoyed the book, and found it useful. If you've reached the end of the book without doing all the exercises, then I strongly recommend that you go back at some point and do them.

Where you go from here depends on your goals. If this book has been your first introduction to Python, then I have three suggestions for further study.

Firstly, explore the features of the Python **language** that we haven't had space to cover in this book. Python's object system, functional programming tools, comprehensions and exception handling are all interesting and useful topics.

Secondly, explore the **development tools**. Python has a wealth of tools designed to speed up and ease development of programs – things like automated testing, packaging, performance tuning, etc.

Thirdly, look for examples of Python being used for the specific type of programs that **you** want to write – games, web applications, data analysis, etc.

Finally, remember that if you have any comments on the book – good or bad – I'd love to hear them; drop me an email at

```
martin@pythonforcompletebeginners.com
```

If you've found the book useful, please also consider leaving a Amazon **review**. You're now part of the Python community, and these reviews will help other people to find the book, and hopefully make learning Python a bit easier for everyone.

Index

49385602R00138

Made in the USA
Lexington, KY
04 February 2016